Surviving Inclusion

Kay Johnson Lehmann

SCARECROWEDUCATION
Lanham, Maryland • Toronto • Oxford
2004

Published in the United States of America
by ScarecrowEducation
An imprint of The Rowman & Littlefield Publishing Group, Inc.
4501 Forbes Boulevard, Suite 200, Lanham, Maryland 20706
www.scarecroweducation.com

PO Box 317
Oxford
OX2 9RU, UK

British Library Cataloguing in Publication Information Available

Library of Congress Cataloging-in-Publication Data

Lehmann, Kay Johnson, 1957–
  Surviving inclusion / Kay Johnson Lehmann.
      p. cm.
  Includes bibliographical references and index.
  ISBN 1-57886-043-1 (pbk. : alk. paper)
  1. Children with disabilities—Education. 2. Inclusive
education. I. Title.
LC4015 .L45 2004
371.9'046—dc22

2003017238

Contents

Preface

"But you're so good with them, Kay!"

The school counselor, the vice-principal, my mentor—at one time or another, all of them—said this to me as yet another student with special needs was placed in my classroom. My heart knew how to make the all-important human connection with these students who had suffered so much already. But I didn't have the skills, strategies, and adaptations to really teach them. At least, not when I started teaching. Eventually, my repertoire and knowledge base were extensive but all of it was learned the hard way: one mistake at a time. The goal of this book is to equip you with the necessary knowledge to handle inclusion successfully, without having to learn everything the hard way.

Inclusion of English as a Second Language (ESL) students and students with disabilities or special needs is a relatively new phenomenon in education. Inclusion requires knowledge and experience with specific teaching strategies, best practices, and assistive technologies.

Underlying this book is a foundation built on the frustrations felt by many general education teachers who lacked the strategies and techniques to work successfully with special needs learners in the past. The focus will be on the positive. It will not dwell on the difficulties of the inclusive classroom.

It should be noted that this book is not meant as a substitute for the training that should be provided by each school and district to teachers in inclusive classrooms. Rather, it should be seen as a survival manual to use until proper training takes place and to refer to after that training as a resource for teaching strategies. One thing will become clear: these strategies are "just good teaching"—and all students in the classroom will benefit from their use.

1

Defining the Inclusive Classroom

Diverse student population—What does this phrase mean? What mental image comes to mind when you think of the diverse student population in your classroom? Here is how one classroom teacher described her diverse student population: "In my classroom of second graders, I have three ADD students, one poorly medicated ADHD, a high autistic student, three severe behavior problem students, and a Spanish-only speaking student!" (C. Stacy-Thompson, personal communication, May 3, 2003)

Well, that description makes it apparent that we're not in the Ozzie and Harriet classrooms seen on TV reruns, or even the classrooms from the more recent show, *The Wonder Years*. Perhaps that idealized version of the classroom never really existed. Nevertheless, today's teachers face student groups with a widening array of talents, abilities, and intelligences. That 'ol bag of teaching tricks needs to be as broad as possible to meet the needs of all of the children in today's schools.

For the purposes of this book, *special needs students* will include students with:

- limited or no English-speaking ability
- physical disabilities
- vision loss
- loss of hearing
- cognitive impairments

- speech impairments
- learning disabilities
- ADD/ADHD
- behavior disorders

THE *WOW!* MOMENTS

Most of us are more successful each day in the classroom than we realize. It's not realistic to think that we will be 100 percent successful with every child every day—yet great teachers go home each night mulling the not-quite-successful experiences with one or two students instead of savoring the *Wow!* moments. It is important to remind yourself of the things that you know and are already doing well. It provides a positive foundation on which to build.

The need to build a positive foundation is also true when working with students and their parents. Always begin with the positive. Whether the occasion is a parent–teacher conference, editing a writing assignment, or some other classroom occurrence that requires a litany of positive and negative observations, let the first comment that is seen or heard be positive.

Throughout the book, successful learning strategies and best practices will be modeled. One of them, begin with the positive, was mentioned above. To make sure that all these strategies are noted, they will be separated. Each will begin with the phrase *Teacher's Note*, like the one following.

Teacher's Note—The Sandwich Method

To correct student errors or communicate student problems with parents, a teacher has to impart negative information. That information is best delivered using the sandwich method. The negative information will be delivered between two positive comments. The positive comments are the bread of the sandwich and the negative information is the filling. This is a highly effective method of imparting constructive criticism.

This is a great method to use at parent-teacher conferences. It allows the teacher to connect with the parent without raising defense mechanisms.

Students can be taught to use the sandwich method when they conduct peer reviews of presentations or projects.

When used to review graduate-level writing, one master's degree student said this about the sandwich method: "The instructor had been evaluating my papers with a combination of constructive criticism and positive feedback that made me feel challenged to change my mistakes, but not overwhelmed by the task" (S. McWilliams, personal communication, June 8, 2003). ■

CONSIDER YOUR *WOW!* MOMENTS

So in the realm of starting with the positive, think of your most successful teaching experience with special needs students. What teaching practices and classroom management strategies led to the success with those students or those specific lessons? It is helpful to begin keeping track of the strategies, practices, routines, and ideas that worked well for you. Likely, a lot of them are in that bag of teaching tricks you use but some might be rusty from disuse. Occasionally, we get into ruts professionally and use the same strategies day after day. Developing a pattern of reflection on each day's experiences can help avoid those ruts.

One effective teaching method, the K-W-L chart, begins with reflection. Here is a Teacher's Note about K-W-L charts.

Teacher's Note—K-W-L

The next strategy we will use is an adaptation of the K-W-L chart. For those unfamiliar with that acronym, it stands for:

- K–What do students already *know?*
- W–What do they *want* to know?
- L–What did they *learn?*

KNOW–During this part of the technique, students brainstorm what they already know about a topic. This is usually done as a large-group activity with the teacher acting as a scribe but can also be done in small groups. It is important during the Know phase not to correct students for incorrect responses. Write down everything! Later, in the Want phase, the list will be organized into subtopics, but the incorrect questions or statements will continue to be included. Students will discover those errors for themselves later. This Know part of the K-W-L process increases student interest in the topic, activates prior knowledge, and helps assess the background students already have. After all, there is no use teaching them something they already know, right? Or, if the class has a great deal of trouble coming up with responses during brainstorming, they may not have enough background to continue with the activity. At this point, the teacher needs to stop and back up, taking time to teach these background concepts. This is especially important for special needs students who will be lost from the start if they lack the background and vocabulary necessary for the lesson.

WANT—After completing the brainstorming session, it's time to reflect on the results of the brainstorm. The next step is to ask the students what they Want to know about the subject. This allows students to use both higher-order thinking skills and their imaginations at the same time. This section of the lesson can be done in small or large groups. Again, student ideas should not be corrected or squelched. The more questions that are generated, the better. All students should be encouraged to participate. Once brainstorming of questions is complete, ask the students to analyze the lists of questions into subtopic categories. You, the teacher, should state aloud what you are thinking as you model the organization of ideas into subtopics and categories. This "thinking out loud" technique will help learning disabled students as well as ESL students comprehend how the ideas can be connected. It is also imperative to use this oral technique if visually impaired students are in the class. To assist hearing-impaired students, write the subtopics on the board or overhead using different colors and then mark the questions that belong in that subtopic with those colors. Alternatively, arrows or lines can be drawn to the subtopics if colors aren't available. Once the questions are arranged into concepts, student teams can be organized to research each set of questions.

LEARN—After a project, it is important to do a post-assessment to find out what learning took place. During this phase, students look over the original questions they posed to see if they can now answer them. This process of reporting the answers to the questions and comparing them to what students thought they knew about the subject before starting increases comprehension, especially for learning disabled and ESL students or others who have trouble with written language. Having small groups report their findings to the whole group can be a good outlet for ADHD and some behaviorally challenged students. The opportunity to stand up and "be the expert" gives these students the attention they crave for a positive reason. This presentation of knowledge through an activity such as a PowerPoint presentation, skit, or oral report lets the students and the instructor analyze what learning occurred outside of the original set of questions. ■

REFLECTION AND LOOKING AHEAD

By thinking about your *Wow!* moments, you have completed part one of the K-W-L chart. The *Wow!* moments represent some of what you already know about working in the inclusive classroom. Step two is Want. What do you want to know about inclusion, teaching strategies, and assistive technologies? Formulate a list of personal goals and at least two questions that you have about inclusion that you would like to have answered by the end of the book. This will provide a clear purpose for reading. This brings us to our third Teacher's Note!

Teacher's Note—Purpose for Reading

Research by the Rand Reading Study Group, which was reported in the book *Reading for Understanding* by Catherine Snow (2002), states that reading can be broken down into three elements: the reader, the text, and the activity. When the activity is purposeful and motivating, comprehension is increased. This will be especially true when working with special needs students, many of whom are struggling readers (Snow 2002, 15).

Of the three elements, the teacher can effectively control two: the text and the activity. It is important that the text not be too difficult. If necessary, provide alternate material for struggling readers or students with learning disabilities.

It is the activity that really provides the purpose. Students with a strong interest in understanding the material will work hard to comprehend even challenging texts. Reading to be able to participate in a class discussion or to answer the questions at the end of the chapter does not usually provide a true purpose for most students. A student who is taking part in a debate, creating an advertising campaign, or writing a skit will likely feel he or she has a purpose for reading and will be motivated to do so. ■

WHERE TO TURN FOR HELP?

It was one of those days when none of the lessons seemed to work. Students weren't getting it and their frustration led them to act out. The end of the day finally arrived, much to my relief. Shoulders drooping, head aching, the answer was obvious! It was time to ask for help! But where to turn for help, that was the question.

A. Bottle of Tylenol
B. Anybody who will listen
C. Team-teaching partner
D. Teaching friend with similar teaching styles and philosophy

Well, the bottle of Tylenol may have solved the immediate headache but it wouldn't deal with the underlying problem. Anybody who will listen (answer B) might have been helpful, but only if that anybody understood the realities of teaching in a diverse middle school classroom.

Those teachers represented in choices C and D would have been the perfect choice, especially if any of them had been trained as critical friends or cognitive coaches. Many of our fellow teachers lend an ear or a shoulder but don't offer concrete suggestions when the going gets tough. They lack the training to evaluate the situation objectively.

Ongoing support and evaluation is being offered to new and experienced teachers alike in schools where organized critical-friend groups exist. Critical friends can be very helpful in evaluating our teaching and giving us feedback. If you haven't heard of this technique before now, never fear! The key word in the phrase is *friend*! Some resources about critical friends are listed below. If you can work with a critical friend while trying out the strategies in this book, you will be more successful. The feedback provided by an observer, such as a critical friend, is very helpful when trying to improve classroom practices. Many classroom practices are habits that are difficult for us to see and therefore very difficult for us to improve. A critical friend can help spot the practices that are undermining your work with special needs students and can highlight those practices that are successful.

CRITICAL FRIENDS RESOURCES

Redesigning Professional Development. This article was first published in ASCD's *Educational Leadership*, vol. 59, no. 6, by a member of the National School Reform Faculty (www.middleweb.com/MWLresources/ debfriends.html).

Critical Friends Groups: Catalysts for Change (www.educationworld. com/a_admin/admin136.shtml) is an *Education World* article about the program by the National School Reform Faculty (NSRF). NSRF provides training to help your school set up critical friends groups (www. nsrfharmony.org).

How Friends Can Be Critical As Schools Make Essential Changes. Essential Schools.org published this article, which includes norms for working in Critical Friend Groups and a worksheet to guide observations (www.essentialschools.org/cs/resources/view/ces_res/43).

Pointers for Critical Friends: Learning Circles. This posting on the Teachers Network is not signed. There are some very helpful suggestions in this posting, including "Thumb Points for a Successful Partnership" and "Engaging in a Critical Dialogue."

DEFINING IMPORTANT TERMS USED THROUGHOUT THE BOOK

This book may have already used some terms unfamiliar to you. Best classroom practice is to introduce vocabulary before beginning the discussion. In fact, when working with students who struggle with reading comprehension for any reason, it is imperative to introduce vocabulary before beginning the study of a new topic. In the classroom, there are many ways to teach vocabulary successfully. Some strategies and resources for teaching vocabulary are included in later chapters. Most vocabulary-building strategies would be difficult and time-consuming to employ while reading a book. Since it will be important for your understanding of future topics to understand some basic terms used frequently in this book, they are listed below with their definition and at least one resource if you need further information.

ADHD/ADD

ADHD stands for attention deficit hyperactivity disorder, also known as ADD, which stands for attention deficit disorder. There are three types of ADHD, one of which does not show up as hyperactive behavior; for those students, ADD is a better term. Most students with ADHD exhibit hyperactive behaviors in school settings—that is, an inability to sit still for extended periods, fidgeting, and restlessness. In addition, they are easily distractible and have trouble controlling their impulses. Many ADHD students are visual learners and are more successful when the use of visual tools and skills are employed. For more information, see the fact sheet from the Attention Deficit Disorder Association (www.add.org/content/abc/factsheet.htm).

Asperger's Syndrome

Those with Asperger's syndrome have been described as having a "dash of autism." They share many of the same characteristics, including the repetition of phrases or actions and difficulty relating to others. Children with Asperger's syndrome have narrow, intense areas of interest. These areas of interest may be avenues to reach students with Asperger's. Whether their interest is Beanie babies or bottle caps, classroom activities can be planned around the area of interest. Refer to the Asperger Syndrome Coalition of the U.S. (www.asperger.org/asperger/asperger_main.html).

Assistive Technology

Any and all devices that help a person with a disability perform normal actions are a form of assistive technology (AT). This can range from a simple pencil grip to a wheelchair controlled by the movement of a single finger. The pencil grip would be considered low-tech assistive technology and the wheelchair would be high-tech AT. A great starting point in this is the Assistive Technology Checklist from United Cerebral Palsy (www.ucpa.org/ucp_channeldoc.cfm/1/12/69/69-69/1027).

Auditory Learner

Auditory learners learn best when they hear information. For those students who are struggling readers, they have often developed good auditory learning skills as compensation for their lack of reading ability. Many auditory learners refuse to take notes during class lectures or discussions because they need to concentrate on the auditory stimuli. Students with visual impairments need information to be presented in an auditory manner. If you are using visuals for visual learners, also explain or describe the information for auditory learners and for deaf/hard of hearing students.

Autism

The number of students diagnosed with autism is skyrocketing. Autism is a neurological disorder affecting the way the brain processes information. A wide range of behaviors characterize those with autism. Some of these include difficulties handling change, repetition of phrases or actions, and social unresponsiveness. Students with autism seem to have trouble experiencing sensations being either overresponsive or underresponsive. Limiting the amount of sensory information that must be taken in at one time is usually helpful to autistic persons. This may include limiting classroom decorations as well as limiting activity in the classroom. For more information, visit the Autism Society of America's website (www.autism-society.org/site/PageServer).

Behaviorally Challenged/Conduct Disordered/Oppositional Defiant

These are three different types of disorders or diagnoses but they appear very similar in a busy classroom and will be lumped together in the text with the label "behaviorally challenged." Students who are behaviorally challenged exhibit negative behaviors, often without knowing why. These behaviors generally begin early in childhood. Conduct-disordered students have learned that their negative behaviors are rewarded and continue to escalate their acting out to receive those rewards. For example, conduct-disordered students may have learned that if they misbehave, they will be put into a timeout and not have to complete any schoolwork. Students who are oppositional defiant do the opposite of whatever the authority figure wants them to do. These are all simplistic explanations of complex emotional and behavioral disorders. These students require a great deal of attention and positive reinforcement of positive behaviors and are also helped by having fixed classroom routines. For more information on conduct disorders and oppositional defiance, see the pamphlet *Op-positional Defiant Disorder (ODD)* and *Conduct Disorder (CD) in Children and Adolescents* (www.klis.com/chandler/pamphlet/oddcd/oddcdpamphlet.htm). For more information about behavioral disorders, consider joining the Council for Children with Behavioral Disorders (www.ccbd.net/index.cfm).

Cognitive Impairment/Mental Retardation/Down's Syndrome

Students with these conditions have trouble processing information because of limited intelligence and adaptive skills. Tasks need to be simplified and presented in parts rather than as a larger whole to these students. The students will benefit from hands-on/kinesthetic learning and repetitions of the skill or concept. For more information, see the American Association of Mental Retardation (www.aamr.org/index.shtml) or the National Association for Down's syndrome (www.nads.org/).

Deaf/Hard of Hearing

Hearing impaired is not the preferred term for those who are deaf or hard of hearing according to the National Association of the Deaf, so they will be referred to throughout this book as deaf and hard of hearing. There are assistive technologies for these students that include hearing aids and transmitters worn by the teacher. Here is the link to the National Association for the Deaf website (www.nad.org/).

Dyslexia

Many students who are classified as learning disabled (LD) have dyslexia. Dyslexia is a set of disorders that is characterized by difficulties in processing single words. For example, some students see letters reversed (such as b and d), making it difficult to read words containing either of these letters. For more information, see the International Dyslexia Association website (www.interdys.org/index.jsp).

ESL/ELL

ESL stands for English as a Second Language; ELL stands for English Language Learner. Both of these terms are used to identify learners who are fluent in a first language other than English. In some schools, ESL students are placed in a transitional program of instruction until they are adequately fluent in English; they are then placed in the regular classroom. In other locations, there is no separate interim program and students enter the regular classroom knowing little or none of the language used for classroom instruction. There is much more information about working with ESL learners, also referred to as second-language learners, in chapter 4. The *Internet TESL Journal* is a good resource (http://iteslj.org/links).

Kinesthetic Learner

Learners who are kinesthetic learn by doing something or creating something. In fact, most students learn new concepts best if they can experience the information as part of the learning process. Many ADHD and behaviorally challenged students benefit from hands-on projects as long as there are clear instructions and few distractions. Those with cognitive impairments also benefit from working with the concepts in a concrete manner.

Learning Disabled/LD

According to *LDOnline*, "LD is a disorder that affects people's ability to either interpret what they see and hear or to link information from different parts of the brain. These limitations can show up in many ways: as specific difficulties with spoken and written language, coordination, self control, or attention." For more information, go to the ABCs of LD/ADHD at www.ldonline.org/abcs_info/articles-info.html.

LEP

Limited English Proficient (LEP) is another term for students who speak little or no English. LEP is the acronym used in federal law, particularly special education law. The acronyms ESL and ELL are also used to identify second-language learners.

Physically Disabled

Students with physical disabilities range from those who have temporary conditions caused by accident or injury to those with permanent disabilities. For the most part, physical disabilities cause little disruption in the regular classroom except for furniture and room arrangements to accommodate the assistive devices used by physically disabled students.

Visually Impaired

Visual impairments include students with low, blurred, or distorted vision and those who are blind. There are lots of assistive devices and technology to assist the visually impaired student. An excellent resource is the American Council of the Blind (www.acb.org/).

Visual Learner

Visual learners comprehend new concepts best when they are presented in a visual manner. This can be anything from writing words on a board to concept mapping to graphical representations of concepts. Visual learners get some information from reading traditional texts but do better when textual material is accompanied by graphs, pictures, or other visuals. Many ADHD students are visual learners. ESL and LD students are not always visual learners but representing information in visual forms helps with their comprehension of new concepts. Likewise, deaf and hard of hearing students benefit greatly from visual presentations of material.

2

Resources

A surprising number of resources are available to assist you in working with special needs students, most of them right in your school! This chapter will explore the people and paperwork (yes, paperwork!) that can offer strategies, ideas, and support to general education teachers.

The special education process can be of benefit to the general education teacher. It can offer a chance to dialogue about the student's abilities and behaviors as well as create awareness of resources available to use with this student. The time it takes to be involved in these meetings can often be balanced by increased effectiveness with this student in the classroom later.

WHAT IS INCLUSION?

What is inclusion? Is it the same thing as mainstreaming? Good questions! In a simplistic nutshell, here are some defining characteristics for these terms that are often used interchangeably.

Mainstreaming

- An older term originating in the 1970s
- Education of the special needs student centers on the special education classroom. Students may spend most of their day in special

education classes, joining the mainstream only for a few noncontent-area classes per day.
- The intention is to prepare students for the regular classroom curriculum.
- Lessons are planned and provided by the special education teacher while consulting with the classroom teacher.

Inclusion

- Term originating in the 1990s
- Education of the special needs student centers around the general education classroom. The student may leave the regular classroom for specialized instruction but the majority of instruction takes place in the regular classroom.
- The intention is to prepare students for adult independence.
- Lessons are planned and provided by the classroom teacher in cooperation with the special education teacher. While the lessons may be adapted in some aspects, the special needs student is doing essentially the same lesson or assignments as the rest of the class (Alley n.d.; Disability Resources Inc. 2000; Curry School of Education n.d.).

Since inclusion is the *en vogue* term in education, and part of this book's title, it will be used to indicate any and all inclusive settings in which special needs students are under the direction of the general education teacher.

DEFINING THE ORIGINS AND TERMS OF INCLUSIVE PRACTICES

Forces behind the Development of Inclusive Practices

The practice of including special needs students in the general education classroom developed because of two main forces. The first is the very human and real need to be respected and treated with dignity and to develop individual capabilities to their fullest. The second force is federal special education law. School funding for those with special needs is tied to the Individuals with Disabilities Education Act of 1990 (known as IDEA), reauthorized in 1997. This legislation was formerly known as the Education for All Handicapped Children Act of 1975. IDEA is a part of the landmark Americans with Disabilities Act.

Least Restrictive Environment

One of the most important concepts in the IDEA legislation—and one that is misunderstood in many educational circles—is that of least restrictive environment (LRE). Students with special needs are to be educated in the least restrictive environment possible. In general, this is usually the general education classroom. As stated in a DisabilityResources.org website article, "Inclusion and Parental Advocacy: A Resource Guide/Legal Rights,"

> The Individuals with Disabilities Education Act of 1990 (IDEA, P.L. 102-119)—formerly the Education for All Handicapped Children Act of 1975 (EHA, P.L. 94-142)—guarantees that children with disabilities receive a free and appropriate public education (FAPE) in the least restrictive environment (LRE). IDEA requires states to ensure that children with disabilities are educated with children who are not disabled, unless the nature of the disability is such that education in regular classes with the use of supplementary aids and services cannot be achieved satisfactorily. (Disability Resources Inc. 1996)

This information is explained here; links to more information are provided at the end of the chapter so that classroom teachers have some resources to which they can refer if they have questions about the appropriate placement of students in their classroom. The expectation is not that regular education (regular ed) teachers will become legal experts on IDEA law. However, errors in interpretation of this law have occurred, and are likely still occurring, in schools around the country. There may be times when it is helpful for classroom teachers to have some resources outside their own school districts about IDEA and the definition of least restrictive environment to which they can refer. This is particularly important when the special needs student has a behavior or conduct disorder, or another special need that may create a danger to other students and the teacher.

DISCIPLINE AND THE SPECIAL EDUCATION STUDENT

Many educators and administrators mistakenly believe that special education students are not to be held accountable to the same disciplinary code as other students. These misperceptions have occurred because of unclear language in the 1990 IDEA legislation and subsequent court cases.

Congress took action when IDEA was reauthorized in 1997 to clear up the language about discipline and special education students. According to "Discipline and the Special Education Student" (Baker and Taylor 2002, p. 29), "The 1997 Individuals with Disabilities Education Act amendments clarify that the only disciplinary procedure that applies exclusively to special education students is the determination of a long-term change of placement—that is, a long-term suspension or removal to an alternative school setting."

In other words, students who are on individualized educational programs, commonly known as IEPs, should be disciplined according to the same code as any other student. To do otherwise would seem to be a form of bias, wouldn't it? A student who is distracting or endangering classmates or the teacher, and who is on an IEP for behavior or conduct disorders (or whose IEP mentions behavioral components), may need to have his or her IEP reviewed.

WHAT EXACTLY IS AN IEP?

So what is an IEP? Can the general education teacher request a review? What is the role of the general ed teacher in the IEP process? These are questions many classroom teachers in an inclusive situation are asking, so here are some answers. Every student who is receiving special education services must have an IEP. Each student's IEP should be individualized to his or her specific needs and abilities. IEPs are created through a team process that includes special and general education teachers, parents or guardians of the student, and others.

To be placed on an IEP, a student has to be formally identified as having a disability. This can be a physical disability such as blindness, a cognitive or processing disability such as dyslexia, a social or communication disability such as autism, or a behavioral disability such as a conduct disorder. Many students who qualify for special services have more than one disability in varying degrees. The IEP needs to reflect the student's needs and abilities as they relate to each disability. A busy classroom teacher may be saying right about now, "Why should I care about all of this?" Here's why. The IEP lists:

- Strategies for working with the special needs student
- Goals and learning targets that are to be met by the student and the dates by which those goals are to be completed
- Support that is to be provided by the special education department
- Assistive technologies that are to be provided for use with the student. Assistive technologies can be anything from a pencil grip to specific hardware and software for use by the student.
- Other personnel such as hearing specialists, counselors, and so forth who are to work with the student

The IEP should be a living, breathing document that helps guide the education of the special needs child. The listed strategies help the classroom teacher design appropriate lessons for the student. If the strategies aren't working, the IEP may need to be reviewed. Any member of the IEP team, including the general education teacher, can ask for a review at any time. And the truth is that there are times in every school system when overworked personnel aren't providing all the support to the classroom teacher that is mandated in the IEP. That is when the classroom educator, empowered by his or her knowledge of the IEP's contents, can push for the support and tools listed in the document. The IEP is a legal document to which the school system is bound; remember that. Sometimes teachers have to be a bit of a squeaky wheel to get all the support to which the IEP entitles them.

THE IEP DOCUMENT

Here's a self-confession. I used to be a teacher who grudgingly attended IEP meetings, signed off on the documents, then stuck them in a locked file drawer rarely to see the light of day until it was time for the next meeting or evaluation. Whew, was I missing the boat! First of all, I was legally bound by that IEP document the same way that the school district was. My signature stated that I would follow the strategies and procedures outlined in the document. If my knowledge of it was hazy at best, how could I guarantee that I was following it correctly? More importantly, I discovered that it was very helpful to be completely aware of the student's needs and abilities, to know what strategies were designed to best help them learn, to know who was supposed to help me carry out these procedures, and the exact role of the support personnel.

LESSONS LEARNED

Many teachers have resources available to them, like student IEPs, that may be going unrecognized. To think about what those resources might be, here is an autobiographical story from the author for you to read.

Lessons Learned from Joey

My own classroom! After five years of substituting, I finally had my own classroom. Hired by my first choice of schools and into the job I really wanted, I was now a core block teacher in sixth grade.

That's when I began learning. No, I'm not confused; I'm sure that I learned more than the students. My students taught many, many lessons to me and here is one of the best! This is the saga of Lessons Learned from Joey.

Joey arrived just days after my first school year began. A nice-looking sixth-grade boy with dark hair and pale skin, he quickly attracted the attention of giggling adolescent girls. That turned out to be not enough attention for Joey. Calling out witty retorts to my instructions made the class laugh. Showboating on his way from classroom to classroom and on the way to lunch made other students look. Flipping pencils into the ceiling took his classmates' minds off their spelling test. When quietly reminded of proper classroom behavior, he would shout into my face, "Make me!"

It was apparent that I had a problem on my hands.

But what exactly was the problem?

When his mother enrolled him, she had no school records. The office had requested records from his previous school but the file hadn't arrived yet.

In the staff room, I asked around about the young man. His behavior was more pronounced in our core block classes but he certainly was no behavioral role model for more experienced teachers.

My mentor came in, observed some lessons, and noted Joey's behaviors. A meeting was held, set-up by my mentor, which included special education staff and a counselor as well as several of Joey's teachers.

My paraprofessional worked with the office staff to contact Joey's previous schools and locate his previous teachers so that I could call them during my planning period. Phone calls with Joey's mother during this time had offered reassurance but little information.

Ready to tear my hair out, I met with the vice-principal in charge of discipline to determine a plan to manage Joey's behavior. And then finally I went to my principal for encouragement, support, and advice.

Thinking Time

Before the rest of Joey's story is told, make a list of all the potential resources that were mentioned in the first half of the story.

Back to Lessons Learned from Joey

The meeting that my mentor set up got the ball rolling and his files confirmed that we were on the right track. We prepared a series of interventions and adaptations. My paraprofessional and I worked hard to try new strategies and carefully evaluate the results. I arduously documented his behavior as we tried the interventions one by one. The "parapro" kept records as well, which could be compared with my own documentation.

Previous teachers, contacted by phone, offered suggestions and noted Joey's strengths as a student. His mother, who had previously not offered much assistance because, it turns out, she wanted to hide his history, now was willing to meet with us and try some strategies at home. It was the documentation that turned out to be crucial.

The special education professionals felt that a behavior-disorder diagnosis was appropriate but as one of them said, "It's almost impossible to get a behavior-disorder diagnosis once a child is an adolescent. Usually the diagnosis at this age is conduct-disordered at this late stage in the child's schooling." It was noted that his frequent moves had fragmented the special education process in previous schools and the team came to the conclusion that he would have been diagnosed as behavior-disordered if he had stayed put in any one school long enough.

Ultimately Joey was placed in a school-based self-contained behavioral modification program for middle-schoolers. Between that program and an alternative residential high school in a rural setting, things were looking positive for Joey, when last I heard about him.

But this little tale is Lessons Learned from Joey. What were the important things I learned from this first-year teaching experience?

Children enter our classroom all the time, some with more records and history than others. Some have disabilities. Whether there are obvious disabilities or more subtle needs, general education teachers know when a student is struggling and needs help. Where can we look for that help? This is what Joey taught me, a first-year teacher, about the resources available to general education teachers. See if the list you made earlier is the same as mine.

- Student records, if they are on hand, contain a wealth of information. Comments on report cards, test scores, and notes from previous teachers all can give insight into the child's strengths and learning patterns.
- Former teachers and administrators can offer suggestions for successful strategies when reached by phone. Look in the students' records for names and phone numbers.
- The other teachers and staff in the building who work with the student can offer teaching strategies and a view of the child with other teaching styles and at different times of day. Time of day is an often overlooked variable that can be very important. Time of day differences may indicate missed meals, medications that have worn off, or simple fatigue.

- Mentors or critical friends can observe your teaching style and the child's behaviors, then offer suggestions.
- Counseling and special education staff can be consulted for their expertise and advice.
- Paraprofessionals, if you have one, can be invaluable in many ways. Documentation, working individually with a student, and getting records are possible help from a good parapro. Just having a second set of eyes and ears in the classroom can be important.
- Administrators can offer suggestions and a global vision of the child throughout the school.

Most importantly—

- Parents! No one knows this child better. Ask for their view of the child's strengths and their at-home demeanor. Get their insight into how best to work with their child.

And I saved the best resource for last—

- The student! Ask what works for him or her and what doesn't, what would help and what is a hindrance, how he or she feels about various strategies or curriculum areas. The best and most obvious is to simply say, "What can I do to help you?"

The End!

Taking Off the Blinders

That's the end of this tale. How did your list compare to the one in the story? Hopefully you have created a list of resources that includes some things that were not previously on your radar screen. Classroom teachers easily develop blinders. There are so many pressures on the general education teacher in today's world that taking the time to look for resources to help us educate a special needs student is difficult. It does take time, which is a highly precious commodity! The important thing to remember is that you are only one of the people on the team that was formed to help the special needs student in your classroom. Taking the time to look to others on the team for some assistance may save time and frustration in the end.

For more information about IEPs and the IEP process, it is highly recommended that you read the Department of Special Education document "A Guide to the Individualized Education Program" (www.ed.gov/offices /OSERS/OSEP/Products/IEP_Guide/).

OTHER RESPONSIBILITIES

Keeping Records

One important responsibility that the regular education teacher has when working with a student with disabilities is to keep adequate records of the child's progress or lack of it. As seen in the story, "Lessons Learned from Joey," documentation can be powerful. The ten minutes a day that I spent quickly noting "what happened and when" provided a powerful record after several weeks. To this day, I am convinced that his behavior disorder would have gone undiagnosed if the only data had been his assignment/test scores and my memory of his behavior patterns.

Confidentiality

Another responsibility not yet addressed is that of confidentiality. It is important to have access to the IEP, but it must be handled appropriately. This is especially true if teachers are given their own copy of the IEP. Alternatively, the IEP shouldn't be kept a closely guarded secret. Teachers, paraprofessionals, and other school personnel who work with the disabled student are responsible for carrying out the IEP's provisions; they therefore need to be familiar with the document and have access to it for review as needed. Whether the IEP is kept in a locked file drawer in the classroom or as part of the student records file in the main office, it needs to be accessible. When viewed as a list of ways to help a student be successful, it is easy to see why the IEP is an important document.

3

The Importance of Scaffolding

One educational concept that underpins all teaching strategies in this book is that of scaffolding. Scaffolding is a critical part of working with special needs learners. But what is scaffolding?

Jamie McKenzie (1999) suggests that scaffolding is exactly like the scaffolding structures we set up alongside buildings when working on them. He says,

> "Structure" is the key word. Without clear structure and precisely stated expectations, many students are vulnerable to a kind of educational "wanderlust" that pulls them far afield.
>
> The dilemma? How do we provide sufficient structure to keep students productive without confining them to straight jackets that destroy initiative, motivation and resourcefulness?
>
> It is, ultimately, a balancing act. The workers cleaning the face of the Washington Monument do not confuse the scaffolding with the monument itself. The scaffolding is secondary. The building is primary.

It is *highly* suggested that you read the article "Scaffolding for Success" by Jamie McKenzie (available at www.fno.org/dec99/scaffold.html).

WHAT IS SCAFFOLDING?

Scaffolding is a concept that took me a long time to understand so it will be explained several different ways in hopes that you don't also struggle to understand this important concept. Simply stated, scaffolding is all the things teachers do, and all the tools teachers provide, to help learners be successful. At first it seemed like something extra, an additional *something* that needed to be done. Later, the realization dawned that scaffolding was a name for all the things good teachers already do to help students complete projects and assignments. It was an all-encompassing word for a myriad of tools and techniques.

First Scenario

Perhaps a scenario will help some readers understand the concept of scaffolding. Picture a classroom in which a student teacher is beginning a lesson. For the purposes of the scenario, assume that this student teacher is poorly trained and there is little oversight of the student teacher's lesson plans by the master teacher.

The student teacher says, "Today we are going to learn about insects. Here are lots of books about insects. Go read about insects." End of lesson.

Most classroom teachers can now picture the chaos that would ensue. And why would that chaos occur? Students have no purpose for learning, no prior knowledge about the subject has been activated, and other than supplying books and the opportunity to read, they have no directions about what they are to do. In fact, the one piece of scaffolding that was apparently done by the student teacher was to gather books about insects.

Mental Picture

Before reading on, envision how you would have conducted the lesson about insects. Mentally picture the steps necessary for the lesson to be successful.

- Before the lesson begins
- During the teaching phase
- After the lesson ends

Second Scenario

Here is a scenario of the same lesson that would very likely be more successful than the one planned and conducted by the wayward student teacher.

Well before beginning the insect lesson, the teacher determines why it is important to learn about insects and what facts and knowledge students should have after the lesson is completed. Then the teacher designs a project that will get those results. In this case, the teacher is helping students learn about metamorphosis.

The teacher begins with a review of what the students have already learned about the larval and pupa forms and the process of metamorphosis. A stuffed caterpillar is slowly wrapped in cotton batting. The teacher holds up the batting and asks students to predict what will emerge from this "pupae." Following their responses, the teacher pulls a stuffed butterfly, not the caterpillar, from inside the pupae.

Looking at the stuffed caterpillar and the stuffed butterfly, students are asked to note via words or drawings in what ways the caterpillar and the butterfly are the same and in what ways they are different. After a few minutes, each student turns to a partner to compare answers and drawings. Then the pairs are asked to share one of their thoughts or drawings with the entire group.

Breakdown of the Second Scenario

What was done by the teacher to make sure that this lesson was successful? Let's break the lesson down.

Before the lesson began, the teacher:

- Identified the most important learning that would take place—stages of metamorphosis and the changes that take place during that process
- Gathered a stuffed caterpillar, butterfly, and a piece of cotton batting

During the lesson, the teacher:

- Activated prior knowledge and reviewed concepts already learned
- Used visuals (in this case, the stuffed caterpillar, butterfly, and the batting) to assist learners in understanding the process
- Asked students to determine similarities and differences rather than telling them the similarities and differences
- Asked students to use words or pictures to explain their ideas, meeting the needs of more than one type of learning style

- Used cooperative learning by pairing students and having them share their ideas; student pairs had to determine which idea to share with others

After the lesson, the teacher very likely would have:

- Determined if the lesson was successful based on student's shared answers
- Planned a lesson that first reviewed the knowledge gained in this lesson and then built further onto that knowledge base

More Specifically, the Scaffolding in the Second Lesson

Now, more specifically, what were the pieces of scaffolding that helped this lesson be successful? What were the processes and tools identified in the analysis above?

- Breaking down the knowledge to be gained into a manageable chunk—the final part of the process of metamorphosis
- Providing visual (stuffed critters and batting) and auditory clues (verbal explanation) about the process
- Directing students during the work portion to note the similarities and differences rather than announcing the similarities and differences
- Allowing students to compare and contrast in words or pictures so they can utilize their strongest learning styles for the work
- Having students share their thoughts verbally with a partner, which will increase comprehension and generate new ideas (hopefully) for each child
- Breaking the lesson into phases (review and explanation, solo work, pair work, group sharing), then letting students know when to switch to the next phase
- Presumably, the teacher paired the students so that their talents and abilities complemented one another. For example, the teacher might have paired a non-English speaker with a student who is bilingual in the native language of the ELL student.

- Reviewing the important parts of the lesson through the group sharing process by acknowledging correct information and subtly correcting incorrect information.

The Scaffolding in Your Mental Picture

Your own mental picture of the lesson may have varied considerably from the above scenario. It might have included a video of the metamorphosis process or the raising of butterflies from caterpillars. Whatever direction your mental lesson took, spend some time analyzing it now to figure out what scaffolding was in your plan that would have helped students be successful.

IT'S NOT ABOUT SINK OR SWIM

It is very important when working with special needs learners that the teacher carefully scaffolds all lessons. Building in the supports that will help learners be successful isn't cheating! Some teachers seem to use a sink-or-swim method of teaching. Students either get it from the textbook/lecture or they don't. And if they don't get it, they just aren't strong enough learners, so they deserve to sink. Yikes! That isn't teaching!

Teaching is creating an environment in which students can learn and are properly supported while they learn. In the second scenario shared above, students were carefully supported but they completed the learning on their own. To continue the sink or swim analogy, some students might need a lifejacket and a hand to hold onto, others might be fine with a lifeguard watching over them. Either way, they get the support needed to help them swim. It is important to remember that the level of necessary scaffolding will vary from student to student. And for each individual student, the level will probably vary from subject to subject. There is no one right way to scaffold every lesson. Sometimes the scaffolding may be gathering materials for student research; other times it is creating a table where students can write their gathered data. Some projects require a great deal of scaffolding for all students to be successful.

WAITING FOR THE BLOSSOMS

Here is one final analogy about scaffolding. A workshop presenter, whose name I have long since forgotten, was conducting a lesson on working with ADHD students that I attended, and said something like this:

> Think of that student as a flowering plant. Some teacher prepared the ·
> ground for that seed to be planted. Another one planted the seed. Someone
> else made sure the plant was watered and got plenty of sunlight. Someone
> else had to shovel the manure that fertilized the plant as it grew. Finally,
> someone got to see it bloom. Remember, while you are shoveling the
> manure, someone else will get to see this child bloom because of all your
> hard work and sacrifice. And stop to think for a moment, on those rare oc-
> casions when you get to see a child bloom, about all the others who came ·
> before you, who planted and nurtured and shoveled manure so that you
> could see that child bloom.

Sometimes it is hard work preparing the ground, planting the seeds, and shoveling manure but eventually that child will bloom as an independent learner because of the support provided while he or she was growing as learner. Each child comes to us at a different level on the way to bloom-ing as an independent learner. It's our job to help them each get a little closer to blossoming with every lesson we design.

4

ESL Students

ESL students are unique in many ways. Looking at their needs and potential cultural concerns will help teachers plan effective instruction. Having resources that specifically address bilingual education upon which to draw will provide support in the future to general education teachers.

Sitting in an airport lobby, one might hear families speaking animatedly in a variety of languages. Looking at faces, gestures, and listening to tone of voice might help you decipher the general nature of each group's conversation. It is unlikely that specific ideas from the conversation would be clear. After listening to one of those conversations, what if someone expected you to pass a test on what was said?

This is much like the experiences of second-language learners in the regular education classroom. Some of the messages might be understood in a fragmentary way but overall concepts would be missed. Keep in mind that as frustrating as it is to try and communicate with our non-English-speaking learners, it is much more frustrating for them to comprehend our messages. We can at least turn to someone else and be understood; our LEP students often feel very isolated and alone.

In what ways can we begin to communicate with non-English-speaking students? How can we best teach class and help them begin to comprehend the content and the medium in which most of the content is delivered, the English language?

The first and most important thing to know is that the same good, solid teaching methods that work with many struggling students, including LD learners, also work with LEP students. In other words, you often don't have to further differentiate your methods to help your special needs students. The reasons for this include the fact that both groups have difficulty processing language, albeit for different reasons, and that both groups learn well when multiple delivery methods are used. For example, when the message is delivered with visuals, or the activity includes a hands-on or kinesthetic approach, comprehension will be increased for both LD learners and LEP students.

That doesn't mean that ESL learners are exactly the same as other groups of learners. In fact, that is why there is a separate chapter in this book specifically for working with second-language students. Let's consider some of the special considerations for working with these students, beginning with culture.

IMPACTS OF DIFFERING CULTURES IN THE CLASSROOM

Late November or early December, the exodus begins from area schools in eastern Washington State. Families, often giving the school only a day or two's notice requesting assignments for a month or more, take off to spend Christmas in Mexico with family. Driving all day and all night, they will make the trip in only a few days. There they will stay until mid-January before making the drive back to Washington State.

Teachers in staff rooms all over the area shake their heads at losing all these students for as much as two to three months of the school year.

"What are their parents thinking?"

"Don't they know how much learning their children will miss?"

"They'll be so far behind when they get back, how can we ever hope to help them catch up in reading and math?"

"Obviously their parents don't value education. If they did, they would wait until school ends for Christmas vacation before leaving and be back in January when school starts again!"

All of the statements above have been repeated time and again in school after school. These are teachers who deeply care about educating each and every child in their classroom. However, if they believe that these parents don't value education, they're wrong! It's just that these parents value family above everything else, even education. Connecting with family is more important than education. It's a matter of cultural perspective. This is just one example of the kind of cultural misunderstanding that frequently occurs in the school setting.

There are myriad ways in which culture plays a part in communication with our students and their parents. For those who have recently immigrated to our country, especially for those who don't speak English, everything is different, confusing, and often very disconcerting. The Help! Kit (ESCORT 1998) lists four phases newcomers go through:

1. Arrival/survival
2. Culture shock
3. Coping
4. Acculturation

The important thing to remember is that students and parents are struggling to understand not only the language being spoken around them but the culture of the new place in which they are living, particularly the social/societal norms that apply in this new place.

Many cultural norms from other cultures may appear in the American classroom to be disrespectful actions or show a lack of comprehension for the material. It is important that teachers educate themselves about the culture of the second-language student. Simple nonverbal communications such as appropriate eye contact, touching, and physical space vary greatly between cultures. A terrific resource that outlines these cultural norms and how they affect the classroom is "Communication Patterns and Assumptions of Differing Cultural Groups in the United States" (Adams, Elliott, and Sockalingam 1999).

There will undoubtedly be faux pas that occur when communicating with the LEP student and parents. Awareness of cultural norms will help but some will be simple communication or translation errors. It is very important that teachers look for nonverbal clues that the communication has been misinterpreted to prevent compounding the mistake. Still, there will be lessons learned the hard way. Here is a story about a lesson that I could have learned the hard way.

A Ms. Is Not Always a Señorita

The foresight of a fellow teacher to include cultural differences in our Spanish for Teachers class saved me from what would have been a horribly embarrassing mistake.

In our culture, the titles Mrs., Ms., and Miss are now loosely used. Married women can generally be referred to as Mrs. or Ms. without any embarrassment; likewise, unmarried women are referred to either as Ms. or Miss without concern.

During Spanish class, someone referred to our instructor, a divorced mother of two, as Señorita, thinking that she was no longer married so she was not a Señora. She corrected the speaker saying that she was definitely a Señora. She then explained that the difference between Señorita and Señora in Hispanic cultures isn't really marital status, as we all presumed. It refers to whether or not a woman has given birth to a child, and more specifically to whether she is a virgin or not! She suggested that if we knew nothing about a woman that we always refer to her as a Señorita; however, if we knew she had a child, then we should always refer to her as a Señora.

Ever since that Spanish class, I have been very aware that, if I am addressing the parent/guardian of one of my students, I need to call her Señora.

HELPING SECOND-LANGUAGE STUDENTS ADJUST

Welcome

First, welcome the new student. Even without knowing a word of English, the words of welcome, accompanied by a smile and appropriate gestures such as a handshake or a pat on the shoulder, will translate to the student that this is a friendly place and the teacher is glad to have him or her in class. Ask another student, hopefully a student who speaks the newcomer's native language, to act as a guide. If a same-language student isn't available, select a student who is naturally expressive—not your class clown but a student who talks with his or her hands and has animated facial expressions. These clues will help the new student understand things better than if a shy, quiet, reserved student is selected. A lot can be learned through gestures. In fact, it is highly recommended that the teacher become extra-animated and use lots of gestures too!

Getting Settled

Make sure the new student is shown the everyday things all students need to access in the room and around the school, including the locations of equipment and supplies such as the pencil sharpener, the restroom and the routine for checking out of the classroom to go to the restroom, the cafeteria and how to get school lunch, and so on. These are all things that should naturally be shown to any new student. It is important to remember, though, that this new student, unlike an English-speaking newcomer, can't just approach the teacher or other students to ask, "Where is the bathroom?" Extra vigilance is in order when helping the student get acclimated.

The Importance of Routines

Second-language learners will settle in more easily if there is a routine followed during the day. It is important to have routines for many of the other special needs students as well. Students with autism, Asperger's syndrome, and behavior disorders, in particular, have a great deal of trouble if the daily routine is changed. For the benefit of all of the students, having routines that are consistently followed is important. This doesn't mean students need to march like little soldiers though.

Once students know the routines, they will often become teacher's helpers because they know what is going to happen next. This will also be a benefit when a substitute teacher or visitor is in the classroom. Students well trained in the daily routines are less likely to get off track when a substitute is in the classroom. In summary, develop patterns for the daily tasks of the classroom and stick to them.

Clear Communications

Second-language learners have to simultaneously translate communications from English into their first language while learning new information. It is especially important that the communications be as clear as possible. This means that the teacher should write legibly whenever notes or messages are written for the class. This will also benefit visually impaired students. The teacher should slow down his or her rate of speech and enunciate clearly. Use a normal tone of voice and intonation while speaking slowly and clearly. This will be of help to deaf and hard of hearing students as well. It can also be beneficial with ADHD students. Whenever possible, have another student translate information into the second-language student's native language. There are also some electronic tools that can be of help in this regard. The Superpen from Wizcom is a handheld scanner that can be used to scan text materials and translate them into another language. (To find out more about this device, visit www.wizcomtech.com/products2/qlsuperpen.php3.) Other electronic tools are featured in chapter 7.

What Are the Critical Parts of the Curriculum?

ESL students, even those who have been in bilingual education programs, inevitably miss part of the content in every lesson. Much of their time and effort is going into translating information from one language to another. That is time and effort that English-speaking students are putting into understanding the new concepts.

It is important that the teacher identify in advance the most critical parts of the curriculum. What vocabulary words and concepts must be learned in order for the student to be successful in the lesson and build their knowledge base in this curriculum area? Once those words/concepts are identified, the teacher should preteach them prior to the start of the lesson, should highlight them during the lesson, and should review them with students at the end of the lesson. This approach will help ensure that second-language learners have had time to translate the information and absorb its importance. This will also be helpful to students with cognitive impairments who often need to hear things several times, ADHD students who become distracted during instruction and may need the repetition to ensure that the information is understood, and LD students who may be struggling with learning new concepts, especially if part of the lesson involves written material.

COOPERATIVE LEARNING

Group work or cooperative learning groups can be of great benefit to second-language learners. If another speaker of the same language is available, make sure the bilingual student is grouped with the ESL student. Research has shown there are lots of reasons why cooperative learning is beneficial for ESL students. These include

- A more conversational language used in the cooperative group compared to the language used during classroom instruction
- A relaxed atmosphere when grouped with peers, which allows the second-language learner to begin trying out English skills without the whole group listening
- Hands-on kinesthetic tasks that utilize other intelligences (Eastern Stream Center on Resources and Training [ESCORT] 2001; California Department of Education 2003)

More information on successfully implementing cooperative learning in the classroom is shared in chapter 6.

BENEFITS OF BILINGUALISM

These students have a lot of strengths to offer in the classroom. Many of us, including myself, sometimes view students for what they can't do, instead of what they can! Of course, that is because the things a teacher must help a student work on are the things that a student can't yet do or doesn't yet know. Those things that are on the positive side of the equation are the achieved goals.

Keep in mind, bilingual/ESL students come to us with the ability to speak a language besides English; some are already at work learning their second language. In addition to helping them learn English, have the LEP students teach others their language. Most of them have lived in other parts of the world; ask them to share their experiences and items from their culture. These are just a few of the strengths these students bring to the classroom. Many of these students will have a bright employment future because they are bilingual. Workers who are bilingual or bicultural are in high demand in many areas.

ADDITIONAL RESOURCES

This chapter is not meant to be an all-inclusive treatise on working with second-language learners. There are many fine resources that should be consulted, in addition to this book. First of all, there are resources in the school and community. Ask for help from bilingual or ESL instructors and aides. Locate community members versed in the student's native language to help with translation or to do volunteer work in the classroom. Be sure to ask what resources they find valuable when working with non-English speakers. What websites, books, or software do they recommend? Don't forget to ask these individuals what strengths non-English-speaking families have brought to the community.

Along with the resources listed in the reference list, it is suggested that the following be accessed.

Lesson materials for less commonly taught languages. This resource from UCLA is terrific if the language the ESL student speaks is less common. The list of available languages includes everything from Afrikaans to Zulu with scores of languages in between. A variety of types of material written at differing levels are available on this site (www.lmp.ucla.edu/).

Meeting the needs of second language learners: An educator's guide by Judith Lessow-Hurley.

A manual for writing center tutors: ESL strategies by Virginia Bower, Charlene Kiser, Kim McMurtry, Ellen Millsaps, and Katherine Vande Brake (www.montreat.edu/tutor/9.htm).

Common problems and complaints expressed by teachers of LEP and former LEP students: Suggestions and solutions by John Gulack and Sandy Silverstein (www.csupomona.edu/~tassi/sdaie.htm).

5

The Web Is a Fabulous Resource

Most teachers have discovered that the web is an incredible research resource for students and teachers. A wealth of information is available on any subject imaginable. So it should come as no surprise that the Internet has vast resources to assist teachers in inclusive classrooms. What kinds of information? Where should a teacher begin to look? Those are the questions, right?

THREE CATEGORIES OF WEB-BASED RESOURCES

Three main categories of web-based resources will be described in this chapter. They are:

1. Information resources about disabilities. Many of the major disability organizations have websites that feature information about appropriate schooling techniques and suggested adaptations. Although much of this information is aimed at the parents of disabled students, it can be helpful to the general classroom teacher.
2. Communication tools that connect teachers to a whole world of experience and support.
3. Portals (sites that have collections of links to other sites) to broaden the research base about disabilities or to find lesson plans and other teacher tools, such as interactive online remediation activities. An

additional category of assistive technology sites is included in chapter 7.

USING DISABILITY ORGANIZATION SITES

Most major disability categories have organizations devoted to supporting those with that disability as well as those who live and work with individuals with that disability. One major site for each disability category is listed in chapter 1. The websites for these organizations are terrific resources for teachers. In fact, many of them have sections specifically for education. Most of these sites also have resource lists that can be used to find additional websites devoted to helping an individual in that disability category. In addition to finding links on the resource page, there are some simple Internet searching techniques described later in this chapter that will allow you to maximize your online search time.

COMMUNICATION TOOLS

Feelings of Isolation Are Common

Information is a great thing for teachers, but many of us need opportunities to discuss our challenges and celebrate our successes with other teachers. While that opportunity to communicate with teaching peers locally may be available in the building, oftentimes what teachers relate is that they don't have those peers available for a variety of reasons. Teachers often report feeling isolated. I know I did!

As an educator with combined interests in online learning and professional development, the small town of Walla Walla has often been quite confining. Few people in my building had heard of online learning, much less experienced it. In the whole district, there was one other educator with whom I could share my interests. Once online, though, there were hundreds or thousands of educators with the same interests. Feeling isolated is not an uncommon feeling for many educators. There are ways to break out of that isolation. Going online is one of them!

Reasons to Try Online Communication Tools

Having students with special needs in our classes is just one of the many reasons to seek out an online community of teachers, but it may be one of the best. Although each student is unique, other teachers may have experienced similar challenges and have great ideas and solutions to share. For those who live in small communities, with fewer resource people to whom they can turn, an online resource may be invaluable.

Most teachers have heard of online chat rooms, message/bulletin boards, or listservs, yet many teachers haven't experienced any of these Internet communication tools. This is quite likely because online communication tools, chat rooms in particular, have an unsavory reputation. Some tools, again especially chat rooms, deserve those reputations. However, there are secure sites devoted to education and teaching that have communication tools strictly for teachers who want to connect with other teachers. The sites usually require a free registration process that deters students and others unconnected with teaching from entering. Teachers who haven't tried an online teacher chat room, listserv, or education-oriented bulletin board have been missing out on a chance to share ideas, concerns, resources, and triumphs with teachers all over the globe.

I can hear you saying, "But what exactly are online bulletin boards, chat rooms, and so on?" Here are some answers to that very question! The tools are divided into synchronous (meaning all parties who are participating have to be online at the same time) and asynchronous (meaning everyone does *not* have to be online at a particular time to be part of the communication). Asynchronous communication tools are especially helpful if the group is scattered around the globe. No one wants to get up at 2 A.M. to discuss a classroom problem. Even time zone differences in a country the size of the United States can make it a challenge to participate in synchronous discussions. When one teacher is leaving school for the day in California, teachers in Kansas City may be taking their own children to after-school activities, teachers in Hawaii are still in the middle of their school day, and teachers near Washington, D.C., are preparing dinner and helping children with homework. It is quickly apparent that finding the perfect time for a chat or instant messaging session might be a challenge.

Asynchronous Tools

Online Bulletin Boards

Online bulletin boards offer one way to get questions answered that are beyond the expertise of the professionals in your school or district. A bulletin board is just like its name implies, it's a place to leave and receive messages. Many bulletin boards are moderated. This means someone monitors the information posted on the site to prevent commercial or other types of inappropriate messages from being posted. Each new idea or question posted to the board is commonly called a thread. Participants can respond to any of the postings in a thread or start a new thread.

Bulletin boards have the advantage of being a public forum. Anyone with an interest or question may post a message. Some boards do require that you set up a log-in name and password, but this is usually a free process and is available to anyone. It does help deter unwanted parties from logging in. Part of registering involves picking a screen name and log-in password. This allows users to log in anonymously if they choose screen names other than their own names. This anonymity can provide the security necessary to discuss things openly with others on the bulletin board. The answers are posted publicly by anyone who chooses to reply. This public posting gives those with the same question an opportunity to get answers without posting the question themselves. Bulletin boards are a type of asynchronous communication. Everyone does *not* need to be on-line at the same time for the communication to occur. Some of the bulletin boards are specifically for teachers; others are categorized by disability type.

One great bulletin board site for teachers in inclusive classrooms is Closing the Gap. This site (www.closingthegap.com/forums) is devoted to the use of computer technology in special education and rehabilitation. They have several available forums that are described this way, "Share your assistive technology questions, strategies, and solutions with our on-line community" (Closing the Gap 2003). Don't be scared away by the terms *computer technology* or *assistive technology*. Many people share great resources, strategies, and ideas on the site besides those directly connected to technology.

Listservs

Another asynchronous communication resource that teachers in the inclusive classroom can use is a listserv. Listservs are group e-mail services. By sending a message to one e-mail address, that message is delivered to the whole list or group of people. That group may be 10 people, 100, 1,000, or more. There is no upper limit to the size of the group on a mailing list. This gives the benefit of being able to access *all* the people in the group at one time. However, a list that includes hundreds or thousands of people may generate more e-mail than any of us wants to receive. There are many, many listservs devoted to teaching. Most have an area of specialty such as technology integration, preschool and kindergarten teachers, or any of a hundred other educational topics that could be defined.

Some lists are moderated. This means each and every message has to be approved by one person, the moderator, before it can be sent out on the listserv. This weeds out spam e-mail and inappropriate messages. It does slow the delivery of messages though.

The sign-up process is usually two parts. The second step, which requires permission from the real owner of the e-mail account, prevents naughty people from signing up an e-mail address without someone's knowledge.

In the resources at the end of this chapter there is a list of places to find teacher listservs.

Synchronous Communication Tools

Chat Rooms

To participate in a chat, one must navigate to a specific "place" on the Internet. This place is usually just a separate window that has a place to type a message and a screen where the messages posted by others appear. The messages scroll off the screen as more messages are posted. Each message begins with the screen name of the participant who posted the message.

Once logged into a chat room, participants may join the discussion currently in progress by typing their message and hitting the Enter key. The message immediately appears in the window. Obviously, a person could sit and watch the messages scroll by without ever entering his or her own message. This is known in the online world as "lurking." Lurking can be a great way to get information without appearing foolish or ignorant. It also can be more sinister, such as when pedophiles lurk in chat rooms frequented by young people. That, however, is a completely different topic. When using a secure teacher site, lurkers are frequently people like you who are just unsure about their ability to participate. My suggestion is to dive right into that teacher discussion just like you might in the staff room at your school.

Although a transcript of the chat session may be available, for the most part, if a person wasn't directly involved in the chat discussion, they've missed it. Unlike a bulletin board, a teacher cannot participate in a chat whenever it's convenient. Everyone participates in a chat at the same time.

One educator-only site is TappedIn at http://ti2.sri.com/tappedin/index.jsp. TappedIn has regularly scheduled chats with experts as well as available chatrooms for conducting impromptu discussions. Another site with lots of prescheduled chats on particular topics is Teachers.net at http://teachers.net/chatroom/. Teachers.net also has many bulletin boards each devoted to a particular topic.

Instant Messaging

Instant messaging (IM) is another synchronous communication tool that is very popular right now. A piece of software has to be downloaded onto the computer to make IM work. Once a person is signed up (a free process) and has established an ID name or number, he or she can communicate that ID to teacher friends, family, or others who also have this software. (The persons you want to communicate with also need to have software downloaded on their computers for the program to work.)

Both parties have to be online at the same time for instant messaging to work. One party who knows the ID of the other party sends a message or page inviting the other party to communicate with them. This causes a new window to open on the desktop of the second party with the invitation from the first party. The new window includes a spot to type a response. From this point, on it's very much like being in a chat, except it is taking place on the desktop, not in a special location, such as a chat room.

Some popular instant messaging programs are ICQ, MSN Messenger, AIM, and Yahoo Messenger. Some teachers and professors have been holding online office hours using IM programs. Many classroom teachers have found them a convenient way to quickly discuss something with a colleague, sometimes even during class. OK, that may not be a good idea if the discussion is unrelated to school but it would be a quick way to see if a student could have a time-out in the other teacher's classroom. Or a way to get help if a student is having a medical problem.

OTHER WEB-BASED RESOURCES

Obviously, communication possibilities abound on the Internet but there is much more the teacher in an inclusive classroom will find helpful when he or she gets online. For example, there are sites that offer lesson materials in other languages as well as translation sites. Interactive sites can be a very motivating way to get reluctant learners to practice/remediate skills. Free trial offers for great software are available. Lesson plans connected to standards can be found all over the Internet. Textbook publishers often have sites with lots of resources that can be used to accentuate the curriculum for gifted learners who are ready for more challenge or that can be used to simplify the curriculum for learners who need a slower pace or limited content. Examples of each of these are listed in the resource section at the end of the chapter.

Linkrot

The trouble with sharing Internet resources in a book is that Internet site addresses change all the time. One day the web address works; the next day, the web page is gone. Regular Internet users often refer to this phenomenon as linkrot. Sites selected as resources for this book were chosen in part on the likelihood that the links would still be viable long into the future. Still, the truth is, even stable entities like major universities and huge organizations such as the American Council for the Blind reorganize their websites from time to time, which is the major cause of linkrot. If this happens, do an Interenet search for the name of the organization.

PORTALS

Teachers need to find a couple of good education portals, sites that have large collections of links organized into categories, and use them as a starting point to find web-based information. Portals, combined with good Internet searching strategies, will maximize the time spent online and result in the quick location of good information. Some major teacher portals include:

- Kathy Schrock's Guide for Educators, http://school.discovery. com/schrockguide/
- Education World, www.educationworld.com/
- Busy Teachers' Web site, www.ceismc.gatech.edu/busyt/
- Teachers.net, www.teachers.net/

Searching the Internet More Effectively

Lots of precious teacher time can be saved by using good Internet searching strategies. Some of the most basic strategies are listed here. There are lots of good sites on the Internet that explain search strategies. Perhaps you could search for one? Seriously, here are some tips to get those searches rolling.

The first step is to do a better job of telling the search engine about the subject. Search engines will find every instance of each word typed into the search box; sometimes that's millions of sites, or "hits" as they are known. Here are some basic ways to narrow down the number of hits.

- Define your subject: What words/terms are necessary? What words/terms do you *not* want to find? We are going to search for information on the Great Pyramid at Giza in Egypt. Some of search terms would include Great pyramid, Giza, Egypt, ancient, and seven wonders. The more search terms put into the search box, the better the odds of holding down the number of hits and narrowing in on good useful sites in the very first search. If the search turns out to be too narrow, it is very easy to eliminate some of the terms to broaden the search.
- Use a plus sign: Use + directly before a term you have to have, like this:

+pyramid +Egypt. Notice there is *no* space between the + and the word but there is a space before the next word.

- Use a minus sign: Use – directly before a term you don't want, like this: –Mayan –Mexico. We only want the Egyptian pyramid information without getting any sites about the New World pyramids built by the Mayans in Mexico.
- Use quotation marks: Use quotation marks to group words that might logically be found together, like this: "Great Pyramid"—now the search engine will look for those words together as a phrase, instead of looking for each of them separately.

As was previously stated, these are just the most basic ways to expedite Internet searching. Lots more information about improved Internet searching is available. Use the Help menu or the advanced search button in a favorite search engine to learn more about searching effectively.

RESOURCE LIST

Online Bulletin Boards

- Education World—Lots of bulletin boards are located here. One of these should fit your communication needs (www.educationworld. com/boards/wwwthreads.pl).
- Closing the Gap—This set of bulletin boards deals specifically with inclusion and assistive technologies (www.closingthegap.com/ menulinks/forummenu.html).

Lists of Listservs

- AskERIC Teacher Mailing Lists—The federal government site for educational research offers this list of, well, lists (http://ericir. syr.edu/Virtual/Listserv_Archives/mailing_list_subscribe.shtml).
- EdWeb E-mail Discussion Lists and Electronic Journals—The page begins with a brief explanation of how to join a listserv, followed by the list of mailing lists, each with a short explanation (www. ibiblio.org/edweb/lists.html).

Teacher Chat Rooms

- Teachers.net—Over seventy chatboards on this site means that at least one should be a good fit (www.teachers.net/mentors/).
- Awesome Library List of Teacher Chat Sites—Awesome Library is a great resource. This page lists not only teacher chat sites but also sites where students can safely chat (www.awesomelibrary.org/Office/ Teacher/Classroom_Related/Discussions.html).

Other Web-Based Resources

- Lesson Materials for Less Commonly Taught Languages—This UCLA site has lesson materials for everything from Afrikaans to Zulu (www.lmp.ucla.edu/).
- Online Translation Tool/Babelfish—Instant online translator for words, phrases, or paragraphs in ten languages (http://babelfish. altavista.com/).
- Interactive site/FunBrain—FunBrain is loaded with interactive educational games that can be used for remediation (www. funbrain.com/).
- Interactive site/ZoomSchool—This site offers remediation materials that could be printed as well as interactive tools (www.enchant- edlearning.com/school/index.shtml).
- Teaching Strategies: Strategies to Assist Students with Special Needs—From the University of Toronto's SNOW (Special Needs Opportunity Window) comes this web of strategies and accommoda- tions (http://snow.utoronto.ca/best/accommodate/index.html).
- Types of Accommodations—University of Northern Iowa's College of Education put together this somewhat simplified list of the nine types of teaching accommodations when working with learners with special needs (www.uni.edu/coe/inclusion/strategies/types_ adaptation.html).
- List of Textbook Publishers from Shasta County Office of Education— Find the publisher of the classroom curriculum materials currently used and check to see what interactive tools and resources are offered on- line by the publisher (http://bellavista.curriculumcompanion.net/ resources/library/textbook/).

6

Cooperative Learning

How can teachers

- meet the needs of multiple intelligences and learning styles?
- cover all the standards?
- keep kids interested and motivated?
- prepare students for the world of work?

Cooperative learning strategies can help teachers answer all those questions. Well-designed cooperative projects are interesting and motivating for students. The outcomes are often cross-curricular and therefore hit standards in multiple areas. Cooperative projects offer a variety of outcomes that help to meet multiple learning styles. Having students work in teams to complete a goal will give them practice utilizing the skills they will need during future employment.

BENEFITS OF COOPERATIVE LEARNING

Cooperative learning techniques, used properly, can help your special needs learners shine! Cooperative learning helps all students apply abstract concepts in concrete ways, creating true comprehension of the material. For those learners who struggle with abstract learning, reading, or language in general, the jump from abstract ideas to hands-on projects can be the difference between frustration and real learning.

Cooperative learning activities bring students together to work as teams. These are natural times to learn and practice social skills and communication strategies. Character education is naturally woven in as students have to share the workload and rely on one another to complete a project.

TEACHING THE SOCIAL SKILLS FOR COOPERATIVE LEARNING

Making cooperative learning work effectively isn't difficult but it does require preplanning. Activities have to be carefully broken down into manageable chunks. Teams must be balanced in advance to make the environment advantageous to every learner. This section provides the background knowledge to make cooperative learning strategies work in every classroom, with every learner.

Teamwork and the ability to work with others is one of the skill sets that businesspeople frequently mention is lacking in newly hired employees. To paraphrase the message from business to educators, "We can teach them the job but we can't teach them to work with and tolerate others." Bettina Brown (2001), citing the work of Brenda Gardner and Sharon Korth, says, "Although group work is seen as an optimal strategy for many job or task challenges, employers claim that schools have not prepared students to function well in a team capacity. Students must be prepared with skills that will enable them to work collectively with others to solve problems that cannot be solved through individual effort alone."

Most educators work hard at teaching social skills. What's most important, though, is that students get a chance to practice those social skills. A classroom environment where every student is sitting quietly at a desk does not allow for practicing positive social skills. Hands-on, cooperative projects do allow for social interactions. Properly organized, these can be wonderful learning experiences about both the content and working with others.

How do we properly organize these events? A great resource, *Dynamics of Learning Groups: Meeting the Needs of All Students*, lists some concrete strategies for cooperative work (Hagberg 2002). Laurie Hagberg lists eleven steps for organizing group work as you will see in the essay that follows.

Dynamics of Learning Groups:
Meeting the Needs of All Students

Plan!

Start by defining, in your own mind, the purpose of using groups in your classroom. If you want a type of temporary study group, then kids could probably group themselves. If, however, you're planning to have students do projects or review activities throughout the year in groups, structure the groups accordingly to achieve the best possible results for all learners.

Structure!

Organize groups heterogeneously. It's often helpful at the beginning of the term to give informal, yet informative, personality profiles and learning style inventories to help you assess the individuals in your classroom.

Balance!

When you know the learning styles of each student, you can then group your students so that you include an auditory learner, visual learner, and kinesthetic learner in each group. You want to avoid having a group of all visual learners, for instance, to best provide for all types of activities you might choose to do. I have also grouped students with a focus on their multiple intelligences.

Designate!

After observing the personalities in your classroom, designate roles within each group. A personality profile may help you determine which student in each group would enjoy serving as leader, which as spokesperson, which as recorder, and which as helper. These roles are based on Spencer Kagan's Cooperative Learning Methods.

Organize!

Arrange the desks or tables in your classroom in sets of four if possible. Groups of four students function best; groups of three or five are workable but not as beneficial to individual students. If desks are arranged in groups to start with and remain that way daily, rather than requiring adjustment of the room or seats, students become part of those groups and respond naturally and willingly to any group activity you choose to do. This allows for spontaneous group discussions when they happen, rather than deferring a discussion until groups are arranged.

Experiment!

The traditional use of groups is to have them complete projects or assignments together. I prefer to make groups an integral part of each day's time in the classroom. Here are some ideas:

- While reading out loud with students, I pause and ask students to discuss an issue question with their groups. This works well if the question requires analysis of the text, but it is boring for everyone if used to discuss what is directly stated in the text.
- This type of group discussion can be adapted and used during the course of any whole-class instruction, regardless of content area. It can be adjusted to pairs also, and definitely produces better results than whole-class drill of phonics or math concepts and similar activities because it guarantees more individuals are actively involved.
- At the end of class, as a closure activity, ask groups to discuss and create a "Headline" for the day's class session based on what they learned. Then allow time for the spokesperson of each group to share the headline with the whole class. This could be adapted to an "end of the week" or "end of the unit" activity. This also works at the beginning of the period to help students remember what they did the day before so that you can easily continue the lesson.
- Peer response groups help writers and speakers. Use the groups to provide feedback and a real audience for the students. Students who fear sharing their ideas with large groups develop confidence as they share with a well-chosen small group.

These are just a few ways you can integrate groups into daily activity, rather than thinking of them as only useful for completing whole projects or assignments—experiment!

Monitor!

You get to have much more "one-on-one" teaching time with groups. As groups discuss even just one question, walk around the room and listen to the conversations. Students will get used to your "visits" and will use them as opportunities to ask questions that they might not have asked in front of the whole class. This also allows you to give spontaneous and prompt praise when individuals show understanding or competence—you're right there next to them as they achieve. You can also more easily and quickly assess which individuals need more help because you can hear their individual voices . . . or silences; whole-class drill or instruction can obscure this assessment.

Trust!

Believe that pairs or groups will do what you ask them to do. If they don't lunge into the activity, look critically at what you've asked of them. I've found that if my students don't participate eagerly, then I've probably given them an activity that requires little analytical thought (an "answer the questions at the end of the chapter" type of activity) or I have not given them a clear understanding of why I'm asking them to do the activity.

Present!

One of the hazards of group work is grades. Grading group activities often creates more problems than the activity is worth—and what gets thrown out is the activity. Instead, throw out the grades and have groups present or publish their work for the class. Grades often skew the focus of the activity and are very difficult to fairly assess. On the other hand, when groups know that they will be sharing their conclusions or products with the class, they hold themselves accountable and participate.

Change!

I form new groups at the beginning of every quarter. I also try to give students varying roles through the year. These changes develop individuals' social and academic skills as they work with others whom they might not have chosen.

Enjoy!

This is the most important aspect of using groups—you get to enjoy your students because you're not dealing with as many behavior problems. Students who disrupt class often do so because they desire attention; with groups, every individual gets a chance to talk at least once during the class time. Just that one opportunity alleviates the pressure for some kids—they know they won't have to sit still for a long period of time so they relax and participate more positively in all activities. (Hagberg 1999)

COOPERATIVE LEARNING REQUIRES PLANNING!

Is cooperative learning for every student? A qualified yes is the answer to this question. With careful planning and knowledge of each student's abilities, all students should benefit from cooperative activities. The Hagberg article *Dynamics of Learning Groups* was from an ADHD website. Little or nothing was said about the special needs of ADHD kids, however. Why?

The answer is that the techniques that make cooperative learning successful work for all kids! One of the key parts of planning lessons involving group work is to create, in advance, structures necessary for students to complete the work. This is known as scaffolding. In chapter 4, we discussed scaffolding and you were referred to the online article, "Scaffolding for Success," by Jamie McKenzie.

The need to properly scaffold projects and the use of group work techniques are mentioned again and again in the literature on working with second-language learners. In the process of working with others, students who speak little English recognize that they have valuable skills and knowledge to contribute. Language skills will be a side benefit; the increased self-confidence and comprehension of concepts will be the major benefit instilled in ESL students through cooperative learning activities.

Scaffolding will help all students be successful during cooperative learning but some students need additional assistance. For ADD/ADHD students, it may be a quieter, less active place to work with their group to cut down on distractions. For visually impaired students, it may be as simple as using the enlarge feature on the copy machine to make handouts easier for them to read. For students with cognitive impairments, it may consist of having a paraprofessional or volunteer scribe their contributions as they talk.

LIMITING STUDENT CHOICES

One element of planning for cooperative learning with special needs learners is to limit the choices for their project. It is important to give students choices to differentiate their learning but the choices do not have to be unlimited. ADD/ADHD students, those with cognitive impairments, and some behaviorally challenged students need the structure provided by a limited list of choices.

Teacher's Note—Limited Choice of Subtopics

The method below is one example of a way to limit the choice of subtopics. Students like to make choices and are more eager to complete assignments when they can make their own choice. The element of chance, the roll of the dice—adds some excitement.

This method eliminates the problem of groups of friends all choosing the same subject and splitting the work. It also helps out the student who takes a long time to make a decision, which wastes valuable class time. Special needs learners in particular often have a difficult time when faced with too many choices.

There are lots of strategies for helping narrow down the choices, including handing students colored stickers or playing cards as they enter the classroom, asking them to pick a number between one and ten, numbering off, and so on. Any strategy that can be used to help equitably divide a class into teams for games can also be used to limit their list of subtopics for a project.

Here is an example of limiting the subtopics for a Martin Luther King Jr. Day video project. Each student group has a representative roll a pair of dice. Each number on the dice corresponds to one of the choices below. The group can choose either of the two subtopics represented by the numbers on the dice. If a group rolls doubles of any number, they may choose from any of the six subtopics.

- Segregation/Jim Crow laws
- Nonviolent protest methods
- March on Washington, including the "I Have a Dream" speech
- Montgomery bus boycott
- Martin Luther King Jr.'s Life and his speeches, except "I Have a Dream"
- Martin Luther King Jr. assassination and legacy ∎

RESOURCES TO SUPPORT COOPERATIVE LEARNING

All of these strategies are adaptations to the curriculum. As teachers, we make many of these adaptations naturally without a lot of thought. Sometimes though students' needs stymie our ability to adapt. When that occurs, here are some steps to try:

- Look over the IEP—it should list appropriate accommodations for the student. If the accommodations are consistently ineffective, it may be time to have an IEP review.
- Talk to the special education teacher and other teachers who share this student. Ask for ideas.
- If a parapro regularly works with this student, ask him or her for ideas or suggestions.
- Look on the web. Major disability organizations often offer ideas for working with students.
- Ask the student. Most students are an excellent resource about their own learning needs.

GRADING THE GROUP VS. GRADING THE INDIVIDUAL

How cooperative group work is assessed is a debatable issue in education today. Some teachers prefer not to grade group work at all. This affords everyone the opportunity to participate without the ultra-responsible members feeling the pressure to "get a good grade" and without causing undue stress for those with limitations. Occasionally, teachers will ask students in a group to grade, or comment on, each other's participation. Those peer-peer scores are factored into each individual's final grade. If peer-peer scoring or commentary is used, it should be shared with individuals only if it is anonymous. In other words, no student should know which group members awarded him or her what score or made which comments. That would undoubtedly be divisive and make it difficult to get full cooperation from all members of the group in the future.

Each teacher's group grading philosophy will probably vary between projects during the year. It will also evolve from year to year, depending on the personality of the class as a whole and the teacher's growing sophistication in getting the maximum participation out of each individual.

Another consideration is that grading validates the work that has been accomplished. Others such as Roger and David Johnson (2003) suggest that we should only assess the group work if we also assess each individual's contribution. "Since the purpose of cooperative learning groups is to make each member a stronger individual in his or her own right, a pattern to classroom learning is created where students learn in a cooperative group, individually demonstrate their learning, and then debrief the learning in their cooperative group" (Johnson and Johnson 2003).

JIGSAW METHOD OF COOPERATIVE LEARNING

How do you eat an elephant? You've heard this riddle haven't you?
  One bite at a time!

It's corny, it's old, but there's a lot of wisdom contained in that little riddle. Many of us offer the whole elephant to our students but we give them no idea how to eat it. The elephant is a metaphor for a research topic too big for one person to research. Instead, the whole class will work on different parts of the elephant and put together all the pieces at the end. This is a cooperative learning method called jigsawing. After doing many, many jigsawed projects in my classroom, I came up with the following key components for successfully using this technique.

Teacher's Note—Jigsawing

Breaking down a big topic into manageable chunks is the object of the jigsaw technique. Like a puzzle, it gets put together one piece at a time, until the big picture emerges. Here are some hints for being successful with this technique.

1. Have a clear idea of the topic. To say "our topic is rainforests" may be too broad, for example. Get specific enough that the tasks given to the students will be manageable. The "temperate rainforest of Western Washington State" is a much more specific topic. It is much easier to broaden the topic if student research is stalling for lack of information than it is to rein in a whole class and redefine their subtopics.
2. Predetermine the subtopics. While this may be a terrific brainstorming activity (activating prior knowledge) to do with the students, they may not know enough about the subject to get the broad spectrum of subtopics. They also may focus on minor subtopics that are relatively unimportant.
3. Predetermine the teams. The balance of abilities on the team will be better in teacher-determined teams. This will also save face for those children who are left out when students pick their own partners.
4. Set up roles for each member of the team. If each person on the team has a specific job, it is less likely that a few people will do all the work while one person does nothing.
5. Explain the assessment in advance. Create the rubric for the work in progress and for the final project in advance, and share it with the students. Even primary students can understand simple rubrics, especially if visuals are used.
6. Take the time to do it right. It takes time to introduce the topic and subtopics, name the teams, do the research, and put together a project.
7. Make sure that everyone gets to see the whole picture. All the projects need to be brought together in some way so that everyone benefits from what the other teams learned. ∎

Examples of Jigsaw Projects

Here are some examples of how jigsaw projects can be used:

- Roman Empire: Each group studied one facet of the Roman Empire and then wrote their information as a newspaper page.
- China Dynasties: Each group studied a different dynasty and created a web page about that dynasty.
- Tall Tales: Each group studied a different tall tale from the textbook and then presented it to the class. The presentations varied from skits to PowerPoint presentations.

- Civil Rights Movement: The subtopics for this were seen in the Teacher's Note—Limiting Subtopics. Students produced TV news clips that were shown on the closed circuit system during morning announcements just prior to Martin Luther King Jr. Day.

Cooperative learning is highly beneficial and provides an excellent environment for special needs students to work with their classroom peers. Disabled and nondisabled students will all benefit from group work in the inclusive classroom.

Assistive Technologies

Assistive technologies vary from simple pencil grips to elaborate computer input devices and everything in between. It is not necessary for the general education teacher to know all the types of technologies available. It is very helpful for those teaching in inclusive classrooms to have an idea of the possibilities and where to go to find out more information.

To illustrate that need to know about the possibilities, here is a sad, true story.

Some People Have More Vision Than Others

During the first week of school each year, the school nurse delivers a list detailing which students have medical needs and how teachers should deal with those needs. One student on the list was Kevin. The list said he had low vision and to avoid any blows to the head. Well, avoiding blows to the head would be recommended for all students, wouldn't it?!

It was evident right from the start that Kevin didn't enjoy reading class. He dragged his feet getting to class, moved at a snail's pace to get out his silent reading book, and thought up every excuse to leave the room. These behaviors are not unusual among eighth-grade boys, for whom reading seems to be a chore rather than an enjoyment.

The nurse's list had mentioned vision problems. Kevin wore thick glasses and held the book pretty close to his face. He never complained that he couldn't see things, but he did ask to have the instructions read aloud now and then. During group work, somehow he was never the reporter or the scribe. Unfortunately, group work was about all that he handed in!

Almost two months into the school year, a visitor arrived at the classroom door. She introduced herself as the vision specialist and asked if she could talk to Kevin. He didn't look at all happy to see her, but he accompanied her to the back of the room for a short talk. When the talk was over, she asked to stay and observe him during the remainder of the class, which happened to be the last class of the day.

After school, the vision specialist asked if Kevin ever used any of the tools that were specified in his IEP.

"What IEP?" was the teacher's stunned reply.

The student teacher said, "Kevin is on an IEP?"

The vision specialist nodded and explained that Kevin had been diagnosed with a congenital disorder of his retinas during the previous school year when he had suddenly gone blind in one eye. The retina in his other eye could detach at any time and he would be completely blind. The detachment might never happen, or it might happen suddenly, especially if he was struck in the head.

Bewilderment and shock reigned for several minutes as the enormity of the diagnosis sank in. The specialist went on to say that Kevin had had a great deal of trouble accepting his condition. As with most adolescents, he didn't want to appear different from other students, and would frequently refuse to use page magnifiers and other tools.

She explained that he carried a magnifier with him, although neither the teacher nor the student teacher had ever seen him use it. She told them that there were several things they could do to help him, including helping him find large-print library books or use books on tape. When the vision specialist left, the next course of business was obvious. A look at the IEP was in order.

When asked about Kevin's IEP, the special ed teacher said, "Well, it's just for vision."

"Just for vision! He's in our reading class, for heaven's sake! We needed to know this. We needed to see the IEP."

Once the document was in hand, it was clear there were several steps that needed to be taken, including the ordering of a large-print version of the literature text. The special ed teacher said she would take care of ordering it, but she didn't know how long it would take. The teacher and student teacher wondered if Kevin would use it once it arrived.

The very same week as the vision specialist's visit, parent–teacher conferences were occurring. The teacher was ever so grateful to at least be aware that Kevin was on an IEP, although she would have to admit to Kevin's parents that not many of the listed interventions had taken place.

When Kevin's father asked in broken English, this very question, "What have you done to help Kevin?"

The truth had to be told. "Not much!"

Kevin's father wasn't very happy. The teacher knew that he had every right not to be happy with the way reading class had been conducted for Kevin so far. He insisted that they make sure he sit near the front of the class, that they help him find books, and that they make the handouts larger for him. Kevin sat shaking his head, "Dad, I don't want to be different from everyone!"

His father said in a voice firm with love, "You *are* different! That is just God's will and we can't change it! You have to accept this and work harder in this class! You are responsible for this grade and you will have to work to change it!"

Then he turned to the teacher and delivered much the same message. More needed to be done to help Kevin be successful in reading.

When the conference with Kevin's father ended, the teacher was drained. The school's vice-principal walked by and asked how it was going. "Exhausting, that was a difficult conference. We had to admit that we hadn't implemented Kevin's IEP until this week because we hadn't seen it until this week!"

The vice-principal said, "Well, it's just for vision."

"Arghhh!!!" said the teacher and the student teacher in unison.

How does the story end?

Both the teacher and Kevin worked harder. The large-print literature book arrived and Kevin decided to use it, even though it was different. The teacher printed Kevin's handouts in a large font and learned how to set the computer monitor to high contrast. She got paper with bumpy lines so he could feel where to write. She let him type some assignments because that was easier than writing. Occasionally Kevin would whisper a request in the teacher's ear on how to make something easier for him to see. Through perseverance on both their parts, Kevin passed the class and even grew to like reading—well, a little bit.

As the school year ended, the eyesight in Kevin's good eye was deteriorating rapidly. Yet, compared to some of the people in this tale, it was apparent to the teacher that it was Kevin and his father who were the ones with true vision!

BECOMING AWARE OF ASSISTIVE TECHNOLOGIES

Why tell this sad story here? It was through Kevin (not his real name) that my awareness of technological adaptations and assistive technologies developed. For example, changing the monitor settings so he could use a word processor or research something on the Internet became a near daily task. The use of voice-recognition software (software that allows the user to speak the words into the word processor instead of typing them was explored. This choice was ultimately discarded since he spent just one period a day in this classroom. Accessibility was all new territory, and Kevin became the guide.

Every teacher has students who can benefit from assistive technologies to make learning easier and more productive. As a regular classroom teacher, the burden of making sure that all possible assistive technology options are explored as required by law is not yours—it belongs to the special education department. It is quite possible that becoming more knowledgeable in this area will help not only special education students in your classroom but also struggling or ESL learners who don't qualify for special services. Many teachers are unaware of the possibilities or rely on specialists to tell them what they need. As can be seen from Kevin's story, occasionally special education does not offer enough solutions. In chapter 8, some guidance on how to work together with other adults, such as the special education staff, is offered.

Assistive technologies can be classified into different categories. There is overlap between the categories but it will allow a better understanding of these devices and tools to have an underlying classification to which the tools can be assigned.

TYPES OF ASSISTIVE TECHNOLOGIES

Software

The first dividing line between types of assistive technologies is software versus hardware. Software is any program that can be run on a computer to assist a learner. Many commonly used programs can be adjusted to improve their accessibility. For example, on a Windows-based PC, there is an icon marked Accessibility in the Control Panel. In this menu, there are choices that can improve the functioning of all programs. For example, the display settings can be changed for those who have vision loss, and sound settings can be changed to audibly notify the user about certain actions. The functioning of the mouse can be adjusted for those who have difficulty with fine motor control. All the possibilities are not listed here; this is just a suggestion of one place to begin searching for answers.

Many other commonly used programs such as the Microsoft Office Suite, Inspiration, and e-mail programs offer accessibility aids. The best way to discover what a program offers is to open the Help menu and search for *accessibility*. Other types of programs were developed for or are used extensively by users with disabilities. These include voice-input programs that allow the user to operate a program or the whole computer by speaking. The voice-recognition software that was explored for Kevin's use, Dragon Naturally Speaking, is an example of a voice-input program. Voice-input programs are useful not only for students with visual impairments but also for students with poor dexterity. Voice-output programs read the information on the screen to the user. Examples of voice-output programs are JAWS screen-reading software and Write Out-Loud. These are particularly useful for those with vision loss but can also be very helpful to students with learning disabilities, or audio learners. Some programs change the way other programs can be operated—for example, making large icons or "hot spots" on the screen that are very easy to select with a mouse. An example of this type of software is ClickIt from Intellitools (www.intellitools.com/Products/clickit/home.htm).

One of the best software tools for assisting all learners is the concept-mapping software Inspiration. The newest versions of Inspiration include talking menus as well as a huge library of visuals. Many inclusive learners are not linear/logical thinkers. They are quite often visual learners. For them, the webbing capabilities of Inspiration work perfectly to organize their thinking, prewriting, or research. That mind-web can then be turned into an outline at the touch of a button. Inspiration can also be used to create directions that combine text with visuals. For many students such as ESL learners and students with learning disabilities, this provides just enough added information to make the directions comprehensible. An example of a simple set of directions organized as an Inspiration concept map is shown later in this chapter.

These are just a few of the software solutions that can be employed. Selecting the right software or software setting, again, is something that would very likely be done by the specialist. However, the classroom teacher may want to be involved in this research. One good article to increase awareness of the criteria that should be used for selecting software for students with special needs is MultiMedia for Special Needs by Gerry Kennedy (www.edbydesign.com/specneedsres/gerryk/mmforspecneed.html).

Hardware—Low-Tech

Software is one solution for assisting students with disabilities but it does require a computer. Many solutions do not require a computer or any type of technology. These types of hardware solutions are often referred to as low-tech. It is likely that many of these will be familiar to the classroom teacher. This list would include magnifying glasses, pencil grips, crutches, and other familiar objects. It also would include special paper such as that with raised bumps instead of printed lines to assist visually impaired writers. Another example would be colored overlays/filters, which have proven effective with some autistic, learning disabled, and dyslexic students as well as with struggling readers undiagnosed with disability. Many of these items—magnifying glasses, pencil grips, and special paper, for example—could be kept on hand to try out when a student is struggling. Others, such as crutches and colored overlays, should be properly fitted to the student by a specialist.

Hardware—Middle-Tech or Medium-Tech

Solutions that are medium-tech include specialized calculators with extra-large display or keys, timers for helping ADHD or behaviorally challenged students monitor themselves, or amplification systems for the hard of hearing. Most of these will be specified in the IEP and provided by the special education department but some, such as a large-display calculator, may be something the classroom teacher has on hand. One middle-tech assistive technology a classroom teacher might want to have on hand is the Reading Pen, from WizCom Technologies (www.wizcomtech.com/products2/index.php3). This is a handheld, pen-sized scanner that reads aloud the scanned material. It was created for dyslexics and others who have difficulties reading text. Another device, made by the same company, is the SuperPen. This handheld scanner can translate and read aloud the scanned information in the second language. The company has a variety of language dictionaries available.

Hardware—High-Tech

High-tech solutions will vary from student to student and will usually be fitted or prescribed by a specialist. This is an area where some awareness by the classroom teacher may lead to asking the right questions to get things moving but these are not items the regular education teacher will have on hand. One example of a high-tech assistive technology would be a switch used for communication. Switches can be powered by hand, mouth, or even eye movements, depending on the abilities of the student. For both middle- and high-tech solutions, AbleData (www.abledata.com/) or any of the sites devoted to the disability in question are your best resources. Again, these are items that should be recommended by specialists. For the classroom teacher, it is only an awareness of the possibilities that is needed.

PICTURING ASSISTIVE TECHNOLOGIES IN THE CLASSROOM

It might be beneficial to visualize some assistive technologies in action. A mental picture of the technologies at work in the classroom may give the reader a better understanding of how and why assistive technologies can support education. Three student case studies are described to help create this mental image of assistive technologies at work.

Zachary

Zachary is a fourth grader with ADHD. Like most students with ADHD, he has trouble staying focused on the lesson. He gets up frequently, plays with anything within reach, and his legs are constantly in motion even when he is seated. He is a struggling reader. And although he seems to have a real understanding of math when he is questioned verbally, Zachary rarely shows this understanding on his homework papers. He is a talented artist, in particular, he likes to draw basketball players.

Zachary's teachers, both general and special education, have been working to help him stay focused by staying seated during instruction. The teacher explains the directions verbally but also has a visual of the directions using both pictures and text that are shown on the overhead. The combination of verbal and written/pictorial directions seem to get his attention better than the verbal only or verbal-plus-text-only directions the teacher previously tried. The teacher uses the program Inspiration to create these directions. A sample of these pictures-plus-text directions is shown in figure 7.1.

Zachary has a timer on his desk as part of his behavior modification plan to stay seated. The teacher sets the timer during work periods. When

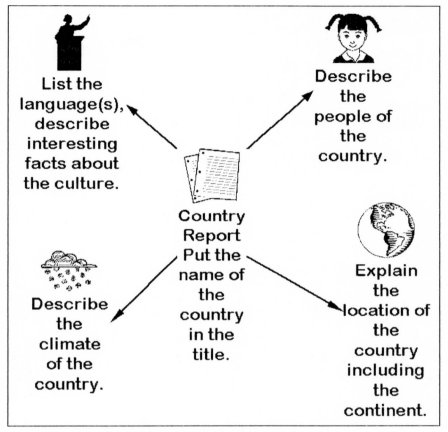

Figure 7.1. **Example of Pictures Plus Text Assignment Directions Created with Inspiration Software.**

the timer goes off, Zachary can, if he chooses, get up to get a drink or move around as long as he doesn't disturb other students. If Zachary gets up before the timer goes off, either Zachary or the teacher records this on a sheet taped to Zach's desk. As Zach shows success staying seated, the teacher sets the timer for slightly longer periods of time each day. A reward/disincentive program has been set up with Zachary and his parents to encourage his increasingly positive behavior.

During any exercise that requires reading, whether it is a textbook or a worksheet, Zachary uses a colored overlay/filter to help him focus on the printed material. He finds that this helps him focus on the words better and his attention span and his reading abilities are improving. He also uses the Reading Pen scanner for some materials and, when using the Internet, JAWS screen-reading software reads the content of the page aloud.

The classroom teacher feels that Zach has a good grasp of math but his ADHD interferes with the ability to stay seated and focused to complete his homework. Zach has been given a voice recorder. For selected problems, he can record his thinking and his solution for the math problem to present to the teacher the next day.

Kyon

Kyon and her family have recently immigrated to the United States from Korea. The family speaks only Korean. Kyon is eight years old and has been placed in a second-grade classroom. It has been determined that Kyon knows and has begun to read in Korean.

Kyon's teacher uses the SuperPen for which the Korean dictionary has been purchased so that Kyon can scan storybooks or classroom materials and have them read back to her in Korean. Korean-language classroom materials have also been downloaded from the UCLA Language Materials Project website (Teaching Resources for Less Commonly Taught Languages, www.lmp.ucla.edu/). Information for Kyon's parents has been translated using the online translator available at Altavista (Babelfish, http://babelfish.altavista.com/).

Shawn

Shawn is an autistic sixth grader with communication difficulties and repetitive movements, particularly arm-flapping. Shawn has been trained to use a PECS (Picture Exchange Communication System, www.pyramidproducts.com/PECS%20Page.html) to make requests and answer simple questions or form simple sentences. ClickIt software has been used to create "hot spots" in certain computer programs to allow Shawn to use simple word processing, story creation, and skill training programs. In particular, Shawn enjoys using Storybook Weaver and Kidspiration.

Shawn's teachers have read some of the writing by Temple Grandin, a professor at Colorado State University who herself is autistic. A particularly useful article was Teaching Tips for Children and Adults with Autism (www.autism.org/temple/tips.html).

Often, the overhead lights are left off and sunlight and low-wattage lamps provide lighting for the classroom. This reduces some visual stimulation that seems to interfere with Shawn's concentration. Shawn sometimes wears a weighted vest (www.autism-atss.com/products.htm) for short periods. This seems to reduce the repetitive movements that occur especially when Shawn is agitated. Headphones and books on tape are used in a study carrel, a semienclosed desk with high sides. The carrel reduces visual stimulation, allowing Shawn to focus on hearing the story.

CONCLUSION

The three student examples hopefully gave some insight and ideas about how assistive technologies can be woven into the classroom. None of the students are real; they are a compilation of student characteristics and needs encountered in the classroom. The best suggestion is to talk with the special education staff in your building. They can advise you on the best solutions for each individual student. In a posting to a discussion in an online course about inclusion, Dr. Marcia Scherer of the Institute for Matching Persons with Technology (http://members. aol.com/IMPT97/MPT.html) and the author of many books about assistive technologies, explained the process of properly matching students with assistive technologies this way:

> It really all comes down to which one (or blend) of assistive technologies will help that unique individual achieve academic success, social integration, and personal satisfaction/self-esteem. From my admittedly biased perspective, the right solution emerges from an appropriate assessment of the student's (and parents' and teachers', etc.) preferences, dreams, strengths and, of course, specific limitations. (M. Scherer, personal communication, 2002)

8

Working with Various School Communities

Inclusion should involve everyone in the school. Students, teachers, administrators, specialists, paraprofessionals, parents, and volunteers all have roles to play in making inclusion a success. Sharing the responsibility for inclusion lightens the load for everyone.

This chapter includes information on working with various school communities: students, parents, administrators, specialists, and the school nurse. Probably for regular education teachers, the most important individuals for making inclusion work are paraprofessionals. Also known as paraeducators or teacher's aides, these are the adults who work most closely with special needs students. Learning to work effectively with paraprofessionals should be the number one goal of regular teachers in inclusive classrooms.

Teachers in inclusive classrooms sometimes feel that they are all alone, like Dorothy and Toto who found themselves in the strange land of Oz. Dorothy and Toto found a team to help them get to the Emerald City, and there's a whole team of people in every school who help make the inclusive classroom a success—although none of them look like a Tin Man, a Scarecrow, or a Cowardly Lion!

SPECIAL EDUCATION TEACHER OR ESL TEACHER

Whichever type of specialist is involved—special education teacher or bilingual/ ESL staff—these are the people who best know how to work with special needs students in general, and usually specifically, the particular student for whom help is needed. There are a variety of models for teaming. Elaine Daack (1999) in *Inclusion Models for a Building Level* summarizes the work of Gartner and Lipsky, "More and more general education and resource teachers are working together using different forms of teaming. A number of these models been successfully implemented at building level in school districts across the United States. Three of those models are a consultant approach, teaming, and co-teaching" (Daack 1999).

The most collaborative of these is co-teaching where the special education and general education teacher form a teaching team to deliver the entire curriculum. Most educators will recognize their relationship with the specialist as being the consultant model in which the special educator meets regularly with the general ed teacher and offers support and teaching strategies. In the teaming model, the special educator meets regularly with an entire team of teachers who work with students with special needs. All the teachers on the team work together to make sure they are consistently using the same strategies and reinforcing the skills taught by others on the team.

Whatever model is currently being used in your school, it is important to meet regularly with the specialists. Be sure to report what is going well with the student and what isn't working well. Overlooking the successes is common; work hard at including this information. Keys to overcoming current challenges may lie in the successful strategies.

Learn to ask for help when you need it! Let the specialist know when accommodations in the plan are not working. Sometimes it is helpful to be specific with an assistance request. Tell the specialist if you need teaching materials, increased planning time with a paraprofessional, assistive hardware or software, or just a shoulder on which to lean.

ADMINISTRATORS

Administrators set the tone for inclusion in the building. These are the people who may be able to provide more resources, increased planning time, planning time for collaboration with other teachers, or staff training opportunities for both the paraprofessional and the teacher. Keep administrators apprised of classroom needs; as the old adage goes, "You won't get it if you don't ask for it."

Administrators are usually very good at public relations. Invite administrators to conferences with parents when you anticipate that trouble may arise. Having an administrator present is a proactive strategy; don't wait until a parent vents. There is a more detailed section on working with parents later in this chapter.

SCHOOL NURSE

Many special needs students have medical conditions that require daily management. More and more medically fragile students are in the public school setting these days. It is important to know which students have medical needs, including medication, that may require attention during the school day. Remember in Kevin's story, told in chapter 7, the school nurse was my only indication that Kevin had a problem—although I was still unaware of the type of problem.

STUDENTS

Those students in the classroom without special needs have an important role to play in making special needs students feel included. After all, this process is called inclusion.

Current Classroom Students

If possible, prepare students in advance for the arrival of a special needs classmate. For example, if the incoming student has recently arrived in this country, read about the home country of the ESL student. Learn and post some words in the student's native language. Children have wonderful ways of communicating without words. Adding a few words from the language of the newcomer to their communications will strengthen the bonds created with their new classmate.

When the student entering the classroom has special needs created by a medical condition, research and read about it in advance. This is especially true if there are some situations that could pose a danger to the special needs student. Make students aware of any medical or assistive equipment that will be in the room. Explain the purpose of the equipment and let students know if it will be off limits. If so, explain why; usually, the reason is for the safety of the student who needs the equipment and the safety of others in the classroom.

Behavior disorders, autism, Tourette's syndrome, and other conditions that can inhibit or interfere with social interactions need very special handling. Regular education students need to be aware of the types of inappropriate social interactions that may occur so that they are not shocked by their new classmate's actions, but they need to understand that they will continue to be held accountable to current classroom standards of behavior while the new student is working toward those standards. Peer pressure and positive social interactions can be an effective element in correcting or aligning the new student's behavior patterns. The key ingredient is information. However, that information should not cause students to prejudge their new classmate or violate the privacy of the incoming student.

Incoming Student

The best resources in education, and the ones that are underutilized in the author's opinion, are the students themselves. Ask the student (any student who is struggling, not just those students with disabilities), "How can I help you?" "What would work best for you?" "Do you have any suggestions to make things easier?" "How do you learn best?" "What do you need from me?" Students are often quite savvy about their learning and working styles. Under the heading of needing any help you can get, this shouldn't be the last choice for information. Listen to what students have to say! This puts them in the position of being responsible for their own learning. Personal responsibility is a goal that we all should hold for all students.

TEACHER'S AIDE/PARAPROFESSIONAL/ . . .

Whatever title is given to your noncertified school instructional personnel, they can be invaluable assets in an inclusive classroom. And it is very likely that an inclusive classroom will include a paraprofessional for all or part of the day, especially if students with severe disabilities are present.

Teachers often don't know how to work with these adults assigned to their classrooms. Little or no instruction is provided in teacher training programs for working with parapros. What is the role of the teacher? What is the role of a paraeducator? What duties and responsibilities are appropriate for parapros? Some excellent resources to clarify these ever-changing issues are the National Resource Center for Paraprofessionals (NRCP, www.nrcpara.org/) and the National Education Association (NEA, www.nea.org/). The NEA website includes a report prepared in 1995 entitled *Paraprofessionals in the Education Workforce* (Pickett 1995). This is a very informative article and it is highly suggested that those teachers who have a paraprofessional in their classroom read at least the sections that define the roles of both paraprofessionals and teachers. In *Teacher and Paraeducator Team Roles*, the NRCP site (www.nrcpara.org/resources/stateoftheart/parateacher2b.php) has updated information on how recent court rulings have narrowed the scope of what paraprofessionals are allowed to do.

The NEA and NRCP articles make it clear that the duties and responsibilities vary from school to school and from parapro to parapro. It also notes that the teacher has some very clear responsibilities. "And increasingly, it is teachers who are responsible for planning, scheduling and directing the work of paraprofessionals and other support personnel such as volunteers and peer tutors. In sum, teachers have become managers of both the education process and human resources who serve as facilitators of student programs and learning." (Pickett 1995). It would be easy to look at that description and say, "I don't have time to direct student learning and the paraprofessional in the room!" It is worth the time it takes to direct a paraprofessional because it means there is another adult in the room who is on the same wavelength, for both instruction and discipline!

Important Steps in Establishing a Relationship with a Paraprofessional

Spend some time talking to the special education department before meeting the paraeducator. Someone in special ed determines the assignments for parapros. Find out who that person is and ask why this particular parapro was assigned to work in your classroom. Hopefully, specific qualities that will be of significant help in the classroom helped determine the paraprofessional's assignment. Ask about the strengths of the paraeducator. If there are particular weaknesses that should be noted, it is likely that these will come up when strengths are discussed.

If possible, spend some time getting to know the paraeducator before the arrival of the special needs student in the classroom. This is a person who will share the classroom; it is vital to establish a friendly working environment.

Ask if the paraeducator has worked with this particular student in the past. It is not uncommon for a parapro to work year in and year out with a student, following him or her through his or her school career. If this is the case, a wealth of wisdom about working with the student just opened—use it! Ask what strategies and instructional techniques work best with the student, and what strategies do not. Find out the strengths and weaknesses of the student. Ask if there are any health or family concerns about which the paraeducator is aware that are not noted in the official student records.

Describe classroom management and discipline philosophies, and then ask for the paraprofessional's help in managing the classroom. This person is truly the pair of eyes in the back of the teacher's head; use this advantage! Remember, it is important that the classroom teacher back up any disciplinary action taken by the parapro. If there is a disagreement about how a disciplinary event was handled, this should be discussed after class and out of the earshot of students. In many ways, this situation is like a marriage. If one partner undercuts disciplinary action taken by the other, students will notice the imbalance. This can only lead to more discipline problems, not less!

Find out what training the parapro has had in the past and what types of training he or she is interested in attending. The more training, the better, for the teacher and the paraeducator. Plan to become an advocate for training opportunities, especially trainings that both teacher and paraeducator can attend.

Tips for Working with a Paraprofessional Day to Day

- Share lesson plans in advance. Do this days in advance—not fifteen minutes in advance—to allow the paraprofessional to suggest and help make any needed modifications. Ask for adaptation ideas and strategies that will make the lesson successful for the special needs student.

- Direct the paraeducator. Tell them what they need to be doing. Many parapros have terrific instincts and will flow naturally to the right task; others will stand back and wait for specific directions. Be overt about what needs to be done and then ask for their input. Before they get to work, ask if the instructions are understood and if there are concerns or suggestions. It is possible that a parapro may see a need greater than the one to which they have been directed.
- Develop ways to silently communicate. It is very helpful to have a signal if one party spots trouble brewing or if a lesson is not working.
- Both the teacher and the parapro should work with special needs students. Every student needs some of the teacher's time and attention. Don't overlook the special needs student who has a full-time parapro.
- Debrief. Even if there is only time to exchange a few words at the end of the day or the lesson, make sure to get feedback on what worked and what didn't.

PARENTS

Parents can be a teacher's best friend in so many ways. Supervising class field trips, organizing class parties, not to mention backing up the teacher when it comes to homework completion or discipline—parents are invaluable resources.

There is another side to that last statement. When dealing with parents who seem adversarial, it is important to always keep in mind that they are advocating for their child. There is no one in the world more precious to a parent than his or her child.

When considering the combined topics of inclusion and parents, it is likely that the parents of the child with disabilities come immediately to mind. There is another parent population that should not be overlooked: the parents of nondisabled children in an inclusive classroom. Parents of nondisabled children can offer guidance and support to their children in learning to accept others and treat everyone with respect. However, to do so may require meetings or literature from the teacher. Be open with parents about the presence of disabled children. Offer facts about the disabling condition without violating any privacy laws and your expectations for the behavior of nondisabled students. Most parents are more than willing to help their children be good citizens. Parents can best do this when they have information that allows them to answer their child's questions. It is after questions are answered that parental guidance in social skills and respectful behaviors can take place.

One of the wisest people in dealing with parents I have ever encountered is my former principal, Jim Sporleder, from Garrison Middle School, Walla Walla, Washington. When we first met, I was a substitute teacher at Garrison, including in his classroom. He was a special education teacher who brought a lot of understanding to the job. Dyslexic himself, he had a difficult time in school and was known to have acted out his frustrations with misbehavior. The principal was honest about that with students. He became assistant principal in charge of discipline in my building the year I was hired. Much of what is included below comes from talks with him about communicating proactively with parents.

- Give parents information. As stated above, don't leave parents in the dark. They can't be of help if they aren't informed. If the phrase "If I'd only known . . ." is being uttered by parents, they weren't proactively informed.
- Invite parents into the classroom and to after-school events. Many parents wait for an invitation; give it to them—especially if the students are middle school/junior high age and above. Teenage students are at home begging their parents not to come to school and embarrass them. If the parent is invited by the teacher, the parent is more likely to ignore the pleadings of adolescents. Once parents have spent time in the classroom, they are better able to communicate with their own children about expectations for behavior, conduct, and homework. Many parent volunteers have said it was an eye-opening experience to be in the classroom or on a field trip with their child's class. Also, parents who have met a teacher in person are more likely to contact the teacher when a problem first arises rather than waiting until it's an unavoidable catastrophe.

- Ask for parental help! This is especially important when the request is for information about how best to work with their children. A parent's knowledge of his or her own child is validated when he or she is asked, "What would you do?" or "How would you handle this?" or "Tell me what I should know about . . ." After asking this question, *listen*! No one knows this child better than the parents.
- Say something positive first. If you have bad news to tell a parent, say something nice about the child first! This helps avoid the "Mother Bear syndrome." Mother bears always defend their cubs when attacked. Starting with bad news begins the "my cub is being attacked" reaction. Mother bears will let their cubs suffer a bit if they know that the cub needs to learn a lesson. Starting with the positive is more likely to bring on the "my cub needs to learn a lesson" reaction.
- Let them vent. Many parents have gut reactions based on their own school experiences. Those parents who seem difficult or reactionary are probably reacting to past events in their own lives. Let them react without becoming emotional yourself. When they've finished, talk matter-of-factly about the current situation with their child. Don't deal with the past issues that they've just vented; work just on the current issue.
- Beat the child home. If a problem of some type arises, contact the parent *before* the child can talk to the parent. For some reason, the first version of an incident they hear about is the one they more strongly believe. Make sure that your version is the first one they hear. Be as factual and open as possible, even if you have to admit that you aren't proud of your own reaction to an incident. That truthfulness will earn you points with a parent.

DOUBLE-ENTRY JOURNALS

One strategy frequently used in the classroom with students is a double-entry journal, which is explained in the following Teacher's Note.

Teacher's Note—Double-Entry Journals

Double-entry journals are also called T-charts. This simple method of taking notes or brainstorming can be used when challenging issues arise for the teacher. The journal can be set up using a table in Word, such as that in figure 8.1 or by drawing a line down the middle of a length of paper with a horizontal line across the page, near the top, creating a large lower-case t; or viewed another way, it creates two columns with room for a header above each column.

When used for students, this can be a powerful way to aid comprehension and understanding. Here are some ways that double-entry journals have been used. In reading, students would label the left side *Questions* and the right side *Answers*. As they read their self-selected silent reading book or a piece of literature, they would note unfamiliar words, confusing passages, or their questions about characters or locations. Later during a class discussion, all of these points would be discussed and the resulting answers or clarifications would be noted on the left side.

During paired readings of content materials or literature, the same chart could be used but with this variation. One member of the pair would read a passage aloud, the other person would write a question about that passage on the left side. Before reading the next passage, the person who read aloud would write his or her answer to the question. Students were taught Bloom's taxonomy and were encouraged to work toward higher-level critical thinking questions.

When students were researching a topic for social studies the same chart, with the headings *Quote* and *Resource*, could be used for taking notes. A quotation from the material would be written on the left, and all the bibliographical information needed for a reference list would be written on the right. ∎

There are as many ways to use this simple device as there are teachers. In figure 8.1, it is used for teacher brainstorming and problem solving about issues dealing with a parent situation. This is one way to take the emotion out of parent discussions and focus on the important question at hand.

Scenario for Double-Entry Journal Used by a Teacher

At a recent IEP meeting, special education personnel recommended that a female student be moved from a restrictive special education room to your third-grade classroom for most of the day. This student has moderately severe mental retardation as well as learning and physical disabilities caused by fetal alcohol syndrome.

Before leaving the meeting, the parents stated that they weren't sure about this change. The parents requested time to think about the move to an inclusive classroom.

The next day, the parents call you at school and begin asking questions: How would nondisabled kids treat their child? Would the information learned be of real use to their daughter? Didn't she instead need training in life skills? What effect might this change have on the girl, who right now enjoyed school; would she dislike school? Would the change be too much for her to handle?

Here is a double-entry journal as it might have been used by the teacher in this scenario, created by teacher Lois McDermott.

DOUBLE-ENTRY JOURNAL

Critical Points	Analysis
Third-grade classroom	Children often establish more responsibilities at this age level as well as social skills
Child is severely mentally retarded	
Child has learning and physical fied challenges	How can the curriculum be modi- for this child to benefit from attending the regular education classroom
Parents are concerned about placing their child into the regular ed. classroom	Understandable that they want their child to learn life skills

Proactive strategies for this situation:

I would answer the parents' questions as best as I could and refer them to some of the other resource people in the district if they have further questions. Presumably, their child could benefit from the interaction of other students in the regular education classroom. The life skills they are hoping their child will learn should include social skills, teamwork, leadership, and so on. These are an important part of the third-grade curriculum. Their child will also receive adaptations and modifications so they can participate in classroom activities and projects. Finally, if they are still concerned about the recommendations, they should revisit the IEP team.

Figure 8.1. Double-Entry Journal. *Source:* Used by permission of Lois McDermott.

The most important point for teachers in the inclusive classroom to remember is that they are not alone. A whole team of people is vitally interested in the success of every child. Learn to ask for help and to delegate—it will lighten your load considerably!

9

Beginnings and Endings

NEW STUDENTS

How often do new students arrive in the classroom? Does it seem like a revolving door should be installed at the school's front entrance? In our ever-more-transient society, it is common to have arrivals and departures quite frequently.

New students enroll in school all the time. Teachers already know how to incorporate a new student into the classroom environment. When that new student has special needs, though, there are additional considerations beyond the normal pattern of incorporation. There is usually a short period of evaluation conducted by special education and/or ESL departments. This is the time during which the regular classroom teacher can gear up for inclusion of the special needs student in the classroom. This should occur before inclusion in the regular classroom, but the reality is that sometimes the evaluation takes place after the student has begun working in the regular education classroom.

It is highly suggested that policies be set up in each school so that evaluation of a special needs student occurs prior to placement in general education. Begin working with administrators and specialists now to ensure that procedures are in place that will allow proper evaluation of all new students, which will allow some time for the regular education teacher to prepare him- or herself, the class, and the classroom for the student. This will work to the advantage of all concerned.

Chapter 9

SETTING GOALS FOR THE FUTURE

Endings, such as the end of this book, give a chance for reflection—in this case, a chance to reflect on all that's been learned and discovered and what changes were wrought through the discoveries. Through reflection, we can see how far we've come and how much we've changed or learned. If you set up a critical friend network when reading chapter 1 of this book, now would be a good time to set up a meeting to reflect and to plan for the future.

As educators, we are constantly weaving new strategies and techniques into our teaching. Either with your critical friend or on your own, reflect for a moment on the learning that has taken place as you read this book. How has it affected your classroom/school/district? What changes did you make in teaching practices? How has your attitude or outlook changed? Ask your critical friends for their observations on changes seen regarding your teaching practices. Ask other colleagues what they have observed. Use this reflection and compare it to the goals you set while reading chapter 1. Also determine if your questions posed when reading chapter 1 have been answered. It is now time to plan ahead for the future.

HEADING INTO THE FUTURE

More important than how far we've come is where we still need to go. Endings also imply the beginning of something new. Educators are involved in helping students plan and prepare for new beginnings. Too often, our busy lives as teachers keeps us from doing that kind of future goal setting for ourselves.

Many districts have formal professional growth plans that include goal setting. In some areas, these are mandatory. In others, the professional growth plan is an alternative to evaluation via twice-yearly observations.

No matter whether the plan is voluntary or mandatory, the features are much the same. Objectives, activities, and assessment are always a part of these plans. Many also have sections for relating goals to standards and tying goals to student achievement or district goals.

The literature on goal setting says: (1) Write down your goals. This formalizes them. (2) Make goals specific. Assessing nebulous goals is impossible. (3) Set deadlines or create timelines for completion. (4) Make goals realistic. (5) Tell others about your goals and ask them to help you assess them. When you tell someone else about your goal, it becomes concrete. When you ask them to help you assess your goal completion, the deadline becomes real. (6) Periodically assess your goals' and set new ones.

It is only through deliberate goal setting and progress toward those goals that teachers, the busiest people on the planet, can make progress in learning new ways to successfully incorporate students with special needs into the regular classroom. Remember to set the sights high. You can't reach the moon if you are stretching for the tops of the trees.

CONCLUSION

This book wasn't meant to be an answer key for working successfully in the inclusive classroom. It was meant to be a survival manual, a life jacket, to help you hold on until real help arrives. The intention was to offer some strategies, ideas, and resources for application in the reader's classroom until the proper and appropriate training for working with students with disabilities takes place. Hopefully this book has done exactly that!

References

Adams, R. J., Elliott, C. E., and Sockalingam, S. (1999) Communication patterns and assumptions of differing cultural groups in the United States. *Awesome Library* at www.awesomelibrary.org/multiculturaltoolkit-patterns.html (accessed April 27, 2003).

Alley, R. (n.d.) *Mainstreaming vs. inclusion.* Youngstown State University at http://cc.ysu.edu/~raalley/factsheetmainstreaming.html (accessed December 13, 2002).

Anonymous. (2001) Pointers for critical friends: Learning circles. *Teachers Network: Reading Room* at http://nsinte1.moe.edu.sg/project/wt/readroom.nsf/f9d1133ff6a5a596482566d90027aba7/9668EE94E1F2370D48256A0D0024498E?OpenDocument (accessed December 3, 2002).

Baker, R. A., and Taylor, J. A. (2002) Discipline and the special education student. *Educational Leadership*, vol. 59, no. 4 (January).

Bambino, D. (2002) Redesigning professional development. *MiddleWeb* at www.middleweb.com/MWLresources/debfriends.html (accessed December 3, 2002).

Bower, V., Kiser, C., McMurtry, K., Millsaps, E., and Vande Brake, K. (2000) *A manual for writing center tutors*, 9. Montreat College at www.montreat.edu/tutor/ (accessed April 17, 2003).

Brown, B. (2001) Group effectiveness in the classroom and workplace. *ERIC/ACVE* at http://ericacve.org/docgen.asp?tbl=pabandID=105 (accessed June 13, 2003).

California Department of Education. (2003) *Cooperative learning: Response to diversity* at http://www.cde.ca.gov/iasa/cooplrng2.html (accessed April 17, 2003).

Closing the Gap. (2003) At www.closingthegap.com (accessed May 13, 2003).

Cromwell, S. (1999) Critical friends groups: Catalysts for change. *Education World* at www.educationworld.com/a_admin/admin136.shtml (accessed December 3, 2002).

Curry School of Education. (n.d.) *Inclusion.* Univ. of Virginia at http://curry. edschool.virginia.edu/sped/projects/ose/information/uvald/inclusion.html (accessed December 13, 2002).

Daack, E. (1999) *Inclusion models for a building level.* University of Northern Iowa, College of Education at www.uni.edu/coe/inclusion/preparing/ building_levels.html (accessed May 31, 2003).

Disability Resources Inc. (2000) *Inclusion and parent advocacy: A resource guide from DisabilityResources.org part II commonly used terminology*, 2000, at www.disabilityresources.org/DRMincl-terminology.html#INCLUSION (accessed December 13, 2002).

Eastern Stream Center on Resources and Training. (1998) *Help! They don't speak English starter kit* (3rd ed.). Eastern Stream Center on Resources and Training (ESCORT) Region IV Comprehensive Center at AEL, at www.escort.org (accessed April 16, 2003).

———. (2001) *The help! kit: A resource guide for secondary teachers of migrant English language learners.* Eastern Stream Center on Resources and Training (ESCORT) Region IV Comprehensive Center at AEL, at www.escort.org (accessed April 16, 2003).

Grandin, T. (2002) *Teaching tips for children and adults with autism.* Center for the Study of Autism at www.autism.org/temple/tips.html (accessed May 26, 2003).

Gulack, J., and Silverstein, S. (n.d.) *SDAIE handbook: Techniques, strategies, and suggestions for teachers of LEP and former LEP students*, 12. California State University, Pomona, at www.csupomona.edu/~tassi/sdaie.htm (accessed April 17, 2003).

Hagberg, L. (1999) *Dynamics of learning groups: Meeting the needs of all learners* at http://adhd.kids.tripod.com/groups.html (accessed June 13, 2003).

Johnson, D., and Johnson, R. (2003) *Cooperative learning and assessment* at www.cooplearn.org/pages/assess.html (accessed June 13, 2003).

Kennedy, G. (n.d.) *Multimedia for special needs* at www.edbydesign.com/ specneedsres/gerryk/mmforspecneed.html (accessed May 26, 2003).

Kushman, K. (1998) How friends can be critical as schools make essential changes. *Essential Schools* at www.essentialschools.org/cs/resources/view/ ces_res/43 (accessed December 3, 2002).

Lessow-Hurley, J. (2003) *Meeting the needs of second language learners: An educator's guide*. Alexandria, Va.: Association of Supervision and Curriculum Development.

Likins, M., Pickett, A. L., and Wallace, T. (2003) Teacher and paraeducator team roles. *The employment and preparation of paraeducators: The state of the art—2003*. The National Resource Center for Paraprofessionals at www.nrcpara.org/resources/stateoftheart/parateacher2b.php (accessed June 4, 2003).

MacKenzie, J. (1999, December). Scaffolding for success. *From Now On* at http://www.fno.org/dec99/scaffold.html (accessed April 17, 2003).

Pickett, A. L. (1995) *Paraprofessionals in the education workforce*. National Education Association at www.nea.org/esp/resource/parawork.htm (accessed June 4, 2003).

Snow, C. E. (2002) *Reading for understanding: Toward an R and D program in reading comprehension*. RAND at www.rand.org/publications/MR/MR1465/ (accessed April 17, 2003).

U.S. Department of Special Education and Rehabilitative Services. (2000) *A guide to the individualized education program* at www.ed.gov/offices/OSERS/OSEP/Products/IEP_Guide/ (accessed December 13, 2002).

Index

About the Author

Kay Johnson Lehmann won the Milken National Educator Award and the Washington Award for Excellence in Education for her abilities to reach every student in the classroom. Her innovative methods utilized hands-on constructivist teaching with technology integration to bring social studies, reading, and other subjects alive for her middle school students. Garrison Middle School, Walla Walla, Washington, with a free-reduced lunch rate of 50 percent and a large second-language learner population, provided plenty of opportunities to utilize the methods shared in this book.

Summers spent working with teachers in the Bill and Melinda Gates Foundation's Teacher Leadership Project along with a master's degree in education with a specialty in online teaching and learning led to working full time in teacher professional development. Her online courses and face-to-face workshops feature the same constructivist, technology-enhanced methods that were so successful in the classroom.

ScarecrowEducation will be publishing a second book by Kay Lehmann in 2004 entitled *How to Be a Great Online Teacher*. In addition, Kay has previously authored two articles and is a contributor to the Microsoft Virtual Classroom Teacher Network.